Love Makes *No* Sense

Love Makes *No* Sense

An Invitation to Christian Theology

Jennifer Strawbridge
Jarred Mercer
and
Peter Groves

scm press

© Jennifer Strawbridge, Jarred Mercer and Peter Groves, 2019

First published in 2019 by the SCM Press
Editorial office
3rd Floor, Invicta House
108–114 Golden Lane
London EC1Y 0TG, UK
www.scmpress.co.uk

SCM Press is an imprint of Hymns Ancient & Modern Ltd
(a registered charity)

Hymns Ancient & Modern® is a registered trademark of
Hymns Ancient & Modern Ltd
13A Hellesdon Park Road, Norwich,
Norfolk NR6 5DR, UK

Scripture quotations are from the New Revised Standard Version of the
Bible, Anglicized Edition, copyright © 1989, 1995 by the Division of
Christian Education of the National Council of the Churches of Christ in
the USA. Used by permission. All rights reserved.

British Library Cataloguing in Publication data

A catalogue record for this book is available
from the British Library

978 0 334 05728 4

Typeset in Adobe Devanagari and Heiti by Rebecca Goldsmith

Printed and bound in Great Britain by
CPI Group (UK) Ltd

Contents

v

CONTENTS

vi

Preface

It is hard to think of a word that sounds more abstract than 'theology'. Lots of people use it to mean idle speculation that is irrelevant to real life. Many more think it is something obscure that only people in universities study. But Christian theology is something different. Christian theology, at least as presented in this book, is far from abstract. Christianity is something real, because Christian people are real. What we mean by Christianity is something that people live. When we introduce people to Christian theology, all we are really saying is that there are Christians, and this is how they live and what they believe.

The Christian faith is something people practise. The Church prays, listens to the Scriptures, celebrates the sacraments, cares for the suffering, and liberates the oppressed. What does this mean for our lives and the lives of others? Each chapter of what follows deals with central issues of Christian theology, presenting an introduction to Christian teaching, but remaining focused throughout upon the lived Christian life. Although this is a book about doctrine – Christian teaching – it is a book that insists that one cannot present a doctrine of the Trinity, or the incarnation, or anything else in the abstract. Teaching divorced from the everyday Christian life is not Christian teaching. However this does not mean that the book is primarily 'practical' as opposed to 'theological', instead, it is to refuse the dichotomy entirely.

Written by a group of priests connected to the St Mary Magdalen

School of Theology, this book is part of the mission of that school to be a network of women and men who read, pray and teach the Christian faith. As such, we seek to offer approachable theological teaching, which is simply what Christians do as they go about their Christian lives. A great deal of it is done in actions as well as in words, in formal settings as well as in everyday interactions, in large groups and in small, with many people and on our own. In all the various ways we go about the practice of theology, that practice is always a lived reflection on the extravagant and senseless love of God. If this is a book of catechesis, of instruction in Christian doctrine, it is catechesis that does not seek primarily to answer questions or satisfy the intellect alone, but to train its readers to live the love and mercy that the message of Christian theology presents to us.

1

Love Makes *No* Sense – Jesus and the Love of God

Peter Groves

Christian teaching begins with Jesus of Nazareth. This simple statement is true for more than one reason. First of all, Christian teaching is about Jesus, because everything about the life and practice of the Christian faith is centred upon the person in whom Christians encounter God. And Christian teaching also begins with Jesus because the first and the ultimate Christian teacher is Jesus himself. The words and actions of Jesus, transmitted to us in the texts we call the Gospels, are the origin and the foundation of all other Christian teaching – Jesus is where we start, and Jesus underlies everything we say and do. So it seems appropriate to begin an invitation to Christian doctrine (a word that just means 'teaching') with a story told in the Gospels by Jesus himself. It is a well-known tale, one you have almost certainly come across before.

The story is commonly known as the parable of the prodigal son, and before we look at it here it is worth asking ourselves a question: do you think the prodigal son actually repents? Luke tells us that:

There was a man who had two sons. The younger of them said

to his father, 'Father, give me the share of the property that will belong to me.' So he divided his property between them. A few days later the younger son gathered all he had and travelled to a distant country, and there he squandered his property in dissolute living. When he had spent everything, a severe famine took place throughout that country, and he began to be in need. So he went and hired himself out to one of the citizens of that country, who sent him to his fields to feed the pigs. He would gladly have filled himself with the pods that the pigs were eating; and no one gave him anything. But when he came to himself he said, 'How many of my father's hired hands have bread enough and to spare, but here I am dying of hunger! I will get up and go to my father, and I will say to him, "Father, I have sinned against heaven and before you; I am no longer worthy to be called your son; treat me like one of your hired hands."' So he set off and went to his father. But while he was still far off, his father saw him and was filled with compassion; he ran and put his arms around him and kissed him. Then the son said to him, 'Father, I have sinned against heaven and before you; I am no longer worthy to be called your son.' But the father said to his slaves, 'Quickly, bring out a robe – the best one – and put it on him; put a ring on his finger and sandals on his feet. And get the fatted calf and kill it, and let us eat and celebrate; for this son of mine was dead and is alive again; he was lost and is found!' And they began to celebrate.

Now his elder son was in the field; and when he came and approached the house, he heard music and dancing. He called one of the slaves and asked what was going on. He replied, 'Your brother has come, and your father has killed the fatted calf, because he has got him back safe and sound.' Then he became angry and refused to go in. His father came out and began to plead with him. But he answered his father, 'Listen! For all these years I have been working like a slave for you, and I have never disobeyed your command; yet you have never given me even a young goat so that I might celebrate with my friends. But when this son of yours came back, who has devoured your property with prostitutes, you killed the fatted calf for him!' Then the father said to him, 'Son, you are always with me, and all that is mine is yours. But we had to celebrate and rejoice, because this brother of yours was dead and has come to life; he was lost and has been found.' (Luke 15.11–32)

Reading that narrative, you may well be thinking, 'Of course the prodigal son repents. He comes to his senses and says "Father, I have sinned against heaven and before you; I am no longer worthy to be called your son." Well, yes and no. That is indeed what he says, but what he *thinks* is not so clear. Try looking at the story this way: the younger son, realizing he has wasted his money and brought himself near to starvation, reflects that his father's servants all have full stomachs. He knows that, having taken his share of the property, he has no more legal claim on his father's inheritance. But if he can find his way into his father's house as a servant, at least he will not starve. So he says to himself, 'This is what I shall say ...'The story doesn't tell us that he has genuinely repented; it simply tells us that he *said* that he had repented, and he said what he said because he needed to eat.

Of course, when he returns home, his father doesn't even wait for him to arrive, but rushes out, and throws his arms around him in love and in joy. The son says his piece, but his father takes no notice of him. Instead, he dresses him in finery and orders up a party. His other son, hearing the commotion, comes in and makes a familiar fraternal complaint: 'It's not fair.' Well no, it isn't.

And that is precisely the point. The love of God, to which the father's actions point, is not fair. It confounds our expectations and offends our sense of what is right and fair. The love of God makes no sense.

This is not so much an exercise in biblical scholarship (interesting and valuable as that would be) as a simple reading of a text. But we can find clues towards that reading in other parts of Luke's Gospel. First of all, we should notice that the story called 'the prodigal son' follows two other stories that concern the finding of lost things: first a coin, and then a sheep. In both those cases, the thing that is found contributes nothing to its finding. It makes little sense to think of the coin or the sheep as anything other than entirely passive in those stories. They are sought out by the one who finds, the one who reminds us of the searching love of God.

The second clue, and perhaps the more interesting one, is contained in the story of the son himself. This is one of several instances in Luke's Gospel where individuals talk to themselves. These individuals all feature in parables of Jesus, and parables told only in Luke. There is the rich fool, who stores up goods for himself in large barns so that in the future he can take life easy: 'And I will say to my soul, Soul, you have ample goods laid up for many years; relax, eat, drink, be merry' (Luke 12.19). Unfortunately for the rich man, that very night is his last, and his preparations go to waste. Then there is the 'dishonest steward' who, aware that he is about to be sacked, asks himself what he can do now he is losing his job: 'I am not strong enough to dig, and I am ashamed to beg' (Luke 16.3). He comes up with a plan to ensure that his master's debtors will provide for him, and he is commended. And then there is the 'unjust judge' who, being bothered by the widow who comes repeatedly seeking justice, says to himself, 'Though

I have no fear of God and no respect for anyone, yet because this widow keeps bothering me, I will grant her justice, so that she may not wear me out by her continual coming' (Luke 18.4–5). (Some who know Greek would translate that last phrase 'so she does not beat me black and blue'!)

The thing to notice about these three soliloquies is that they are all made for reasons of selfishness. The rich man is thinking of his future idleness, the steward of his livelihood, the judge of his peace and protection. None is acting for the right reason. Now think again of the prodigal son. Starving among the pigsties, he 'comes to himself' and realizes what he has to do and say in order to gain a full stomach. At no point does the story tell us that the son repents. It simply tells us that he decides *to say that he repents.*

The younger son is hardly a likeable figure, even on the traditional reading. If we decide that he remains thoroughly self-serving throughout, he is even less likeable. It is hard to imagine a more damning picture of selfishness, and hence it is hard to imagine how one could possibly find the younger son lovable. The actions of the father seem ludicrous. And that, again, is the point. The love of God is ludicrous; it makes no sense. The story of the two sons gives us an unavoidable picture of absolutely unconditional love, love poured out unthinkingly upon someone who does not even begin to deserve it; it is forgiveness offered without question or hesitation to someone who has done nothing to merit it.

This love – irrational, unconditional, offensive even – is the substance of Jesus' story. But this love is also much more than something to narrate. For Christians, love is what we mean when we talk about God, and love is what we meet when we meet the person called Jesus of Nazareth. When we read the Gospels, we will find that again and again the righteous indignation of those who know what is right, what is fair, the way things are supposed to work, comes up against the senseless self-giving love that Jesus teaches and that he enacts. When we enter into the story of Jesus we will encounter a person who does more than teach the love that makes no sense. We will encounter that love itself personified, lived out in the life of a person, and that encounter will change the way we think and act and live.

There are lots of ways in which Christians have responded to that encounter, but all have something in common. To meet the love of God in Jesus is to have our preconceptions overturned. What we think we perceive and understand will turn out to be illusory, because what God teaches in the person of Jesus revolutionizes all we supposed we knew. In the New Testament, this idea is often communicated with reference to the senses. In Jesus, we see and we hear differently. Jesus opens our eyes and our ears to a world of love far beyond the perception of self and me and mine.

One Gospel, John, puts this beautifully when it tells the story of a man born blind who has been healed by Jesus. That man, interrogated by the religious authorities who refuse to accept what has happened, responds very simply when Jesus is accused: 'I do not know whether he is a sinner. One thing I do know, that though I was blind, now I see' (John 9.25). These words are a summary of Christian faith. Jesus is a person in whom everything looks different. By that, we do not mean that Jesus looks different from every other person, though there is a sense in which that is true. Rather, we mean that encountering Jesus transforms the way we see the world, the ways in which we perceive everything there is to perceive. Ourselves, our lives, the world in which we live, all are seen afresh when we come face to face with Jesus of Nazareth. The early Christians articulated this transformation in many different ways, none of which could entirely capture the seemingly endless dimensions that life contained once seen through Jesus. They spoke of him in the most drastic of terms – as like the end of the world, or like its beginning, creation happening all over again. But most importantly they spoke of him in terms of the divine, for they knew that when they encountered Jesus of Nazareth they encountered God.

In John's Gospel, to encounter God in Jesus is to see everything differently. For another early Christian writer, the encounter means hearing everything differently, because 'God spoke to our ancestors in many and various ways by the prophets, but in these last days he has spoken to us by a Son' (Heb. 1.1–2). Those are the opening words of the New Testament's Letter to the Hebrews. In the past, God spoke in many different ways, but now his word, his speech, has changed. To use an awful cliché, 'this time it's personal' because God is communicating not in a thunderbolt, or a miracle, or an altar, or a text. God is communicating in a person.

We need to note a distinction here: the Scripture we call the Old Testament tells us much about the word of the Lord, and the ways in which God spoke in times past. The Church came to identify this speaking with Jesus himself, and so what was the word (lower case) became, in Christian teaching, the Word, not a thing but a person. In the Old Testament we learn that the word of God is something living, which itself gives life to that which is created. God spoke, and it was done. The word of the Lord comes to the prophets and fills them, and manifests itself in what they say but also in what they do. The word and the acts of God should not be separated: what God says and what God does both tell us of the God of love whom we meet in Jesus Christ. However, speech is only comprehensible if I understand its context. If I hold up a white sheet and say 'paper', you might think it obvious. But if you had never heard the word 'paper' before, how would you know I meant that sheet, and didn't mean to convey the idea 'white' or 'rectangular'? I need to know where to place speech, in what context it belongs. If I want to know the meaning of the word 'evolution' I will do better looking in a biology lab than I will looking on a football pitch.

God's speech is another matter. We might think we know what we're dealing with, we might try to pin down the activity of God in a book or in a building, but in all of these attempts we are mistaken, because God will not be restricted. God is always active, always speaking, as we see in the Old Testament. But these words, this speech, is partial. Snatches heard here and there by those who would listen. And so this problem remains a problem: if I can only make sense of words in context, how will I ever be able to hear the word of God? The answer, according to Scripture, is that God speaks God's word in the form of a person, a person who is the Son of God the Father almighty. This will be the substance of Chapter 5: in the incarnation, love is personified in Jesus.

In many and various ways, God spoke to our ancestors of old. But now God has spoken to us in a son. Jesus being a son is a dominant theme of the New Testament, but the early Christians were concerned to point out what this *didn't* mean as well as what it did. Did it mean, perhaps, that Jesus was some sort of angelic creature in human form? No. Being a son is something different altogether, according to the writer of Hebrews. Did it mean that Jesus was adopted by the Father as a response to the wonderful life that he lived; did he achieve sonship through his holiness and obedience? No, because that sort of sonship – in which terms the kings of Israel are often described – suggests nothing of the intimacy with the Father that we see in Jesus. It suggests instead that Jesus was just another very holy prophet. Did sonship mean that Jesus was some sort of conquering hero, fighting battles and returning victorious from military triumph? No. In Mark's Gospel, Jesus refuses to be called anything other than 'Son of Man' until he has reached his lowest point – betrayal, arrest, abandonment and condemnation. It is when he sees him die that the centurion calls him 'Son of God'.

These questions and answers are the stuff of what we call 'Christology', the process of reflecting on how best to speak of Jesus as the Christ, the 'anointed one', or 'messiah'. The early Christians developed their speaking by insisting on two remarkable claims about Jesus as the Son of God. The first of these is the strange idea that Jesus Christ existed before he was born. Scholars call this 'pre-existence', and you will find it throughout the New Testament: at the beginning of John's Gospel, in the writings of Paul who refers to Jesus having been 'in the form of God' (Phil. 2.6); and in Hebrews, from which I've been quoting – to name but a few. Several times, the Gospel writers report Jesus doing and saying things that the Old Testament shows to be the prerogative of the Lord himself, the God of Israel.

Second, and slightly later in the story, Christians came to insist that Jesus, the Son, was 'of the same substance' (that is, the same stuff) as the Father. What was true of the Father was true of the Son. He was not created, but had always existed. This talk seemed strange to many, but to others it was strangely necessary to argue that God had united himself with humanity in order to transform it. God becomes human so as to reveal, in the context of a human life, what true life, eternal life, divine life, really is. Christians found common ways of expressing the things they believed about God and about Jesus in texts that we now call 'creeds', or statements of belief. One important Christian creed uses the phrase 'begotten, not made' to talk about the divinity of Jesus, because the relationship of Father to Son, as well as spelling out the words of Jesus himself in the Gospels, also comes as close as possible to expressing that inexpressible idea of both being the same and yet also being different. The Son is God, the Father is God, the Son is not the Father, but originates from him not as one who had a beginning, but as one who cannot exist without the other.

These reflections on the life of God are basic to Christian thinking, and they will be developed further when we discuss the Trinity in more depth. They centre on the love of God. Love is the life of God, uniting Father and Son, and love is what we meet when we meet God in Jesus of Nazareth. We respond to the love of God and we learn again what it means to see and to hear, and having learned, we think and speak anew. The love of God in Jesus both transforms and challenges us at once, daring to suggest that the safest things of all – the security of my own moral order and sense of personal superiority – are in fact imprisonment rather than protection. In order truly to be free, I am challenged to forget all that I thought I knew and instead to be aware of the stupidity of God's love that enfolds me at the greatest point of my recalcitrance and immaturity. If God is good, my mind rants on, then things must be fair, that's the way the world works. The younger son must not get his fatted calf, the older son's complaint must be upheld. Our offence will, if we let it, rail against much of Jesus' teaching: the workers who worked only the last hour in the vineyard should not get as much as those who toiled all day; the greedy little tax collector shouldn't be the one to whose house Jesus invites himself for dinner. It's not fair, it makes no sense.

Love makes no sense. It is unsettling, undermining, deconstructive. It turns our world upside down, challenges all our preconceptions, invites us to reconsider the whole of our lives now that love has arrived on the scene. The absurdity of Christianity is not just that the love that makes no sense is the truth that we find in Jesus of Nazareth. The real absurdity of Christianity is the claim that that love is what we are talking about when we are talking about God himself. God is love, and love makes no sense.

Further Reading

Burrows, Ruth (2012), *Love Unknown*, London: Bloomsbury.

McCabe, Herbert (1999), *God Matters*, London: Bloomsbury.

Williams, Rowan (2012), *Being Christian*, London: SPCK.

2

Love in Excess – God the Holy Trinity

Jennifer Strawbridge

The doctrine of the Trinity – the understanding of God as Father, Son and Holy Spirit – is perhaps the ultimate example of something that appears to make no sense. One plus one plus one does not equal one in our world. Even when we define the Trinity as one God eternally inseparable as three *persons*, we can only do so with the clarification that *person* is not the same as our modern understanding of a self-absorbed individual. The earliest Christians who grappled with the understanding of God as Father, Son and Spirit describe this oneness both as a marvel (Clement of Alexandria) and as something that cannot be grasped by human knowledge alone (Augustine). In other words, to them and to us, the Trinity makes no sense.

When we turn to Scripture to help us make sense of one God as three persons, we can be further thrown off-track when we discover that the word 'Trinity' is not found in the Bible. Such a reality has led many to conclude that the New Testament writers are not trinitarian. However, while we don't find the word 'Trinity' in the Bible, the scriptural record nevertheless speaks to us of the oneness and unity of God that cannot be separated from the existence of God as Father, Son and Holy Spirit.

Our first port of call in Scripture when we think of the doctrine of the Trinity is most often the Great Commission at the end of Matthew's Gospel. Here, Jesus tells his disciples to 'Go therefore and make disciples of all nations, baptizing them in the name of the Father and of the Son and of the Holy Spirit, and teaching them to obey everything that I have commanded you' (Matt. 28.19–20). Jesus' final words to his disciples send them into the world to offer healing, administer justice, and live out their faith in the name of the Father, the Son and the Spirit. Moreover, and perhaps most importantly, these actions – and especially the act of baptism – cannot be disconnected from God as Father, Son and Spirit.

At the same time, we might also think of the apostle Paul and his second letter to the people of Corinth. In this letter, we encounter another final statement from a teacher to his community of followers. Paul's prayer from 2 Corinthians includes the invocation that 'the grace of our Lord Jesus Christ, the love of God, and the community of the Holy Spirit be with all of you' (2 Cor. 13.13). Once again, those who follow Christ are sent into the world bearing the grace, love and community of God as Father, Son and Spirit. And once again, this language of God's tri-unity is not found in an abstract form, but intimately connected to prayer and community. In fact, these words from Paul continue to be used by a number of Christians at the beginning and end of worship.

While we are right to be wary of anachronistic readings of Scripture that proof-text passages to fit what we now know of later doctrine – such as the doctrine of God the Holy Trinity – statements about God's triune nature can be found across the New Testament. Certainly, it takes the Church almost 300 years after the New Testament texts were written to put into words exactly what the doctrine of the Holy Trinity entails. But when the Church finally uses the language of 'Trinity', the description of God as one being in three persons unsurprisingly draws heavily on the language of Scripture.

Nevertheless, this foundation in Scripture didn't prevent some confusion concerning the doctrine of the Trinity. Numerous wise and educated Christians have attempted to explain the oneness of God through the centuries, and many of them have ended up in a bit of trouble. The explanation that the Trinity is the sun with its *creations* of light and heat is one of the many troublesome analogies where the Son and Holy Spirit become *creations* of the Father (Chapter 3 on creation offers further detail on why God is not a creature). The Trinity as a three-leaf clover, or compared with the forms of water, ice and steam, or like a man who is a father, husband and son, also present difficulties because the three persons are simply three aspects (or modes) of God, not distinct persons. Many a sermon has been preached attempting to explain the Trinity on this side of heaven, and many a congregation has either been lulled into sleep or led into yet another troublesome analogy. For some early Christians, it was better for the Trinity to make no sense, or for someone to have an incomplete understanding of it, than for a person to use a bad analogy to explain it.

This tendency towards bad explanations and senselessness does not sit well with us as we struggle with one of the foundational questions of our faith: How can God be three persons and yet one God? We certainly don't want to end up with another troublesome explanation, but one of the most frustrating answers to this question is that the Trinity is a mystery. This is because calling the Trinity a mystery seems to confirm that the Trinity doesn't make sense and also feels like an easy way to avoid a difficult question. But this is not what we mean when we call the Trinity a 'mystery'.

The language of mystery fills the pages of Scripture. Within the New Testament, we find that the kingdom of God is a mystery; the revelation of God is a mystery; the salvation of all is a mystery; and resurrection from the dead is a mystery. Moreover, Christ is a mystery; God's wisdom is a mystery; the gospel is a mystery; and faith is a mystery. While the Trinity may ultimately be a mystery, it is in good company. Moreover, while the Trinity may in this life not be fully knowable, this does not mean that we can know nothing of the Trinity. Rather, this element of mystery is one of the many gifts given to us by the Trinity.

We live in a world that thrives on five-year plans and, in the words of the poet Wendell Berry, loves 'the quick profit, the annual raise, vacation with pay … more of everything ready-made' (Berry, 2012, p. 173). Thus, not having an answer to the questions about our life, our world and our future can be at best difficult and, at worst, disheartening. To describe the deepest element of our reality, of our God, as mystery can frighten us. Such a description means that we cannot see everything clearly and it means that we only know in part. But Scripture, where so much is described as 'mystery', is also clear that a mystery is not something to which we have zero access. A mystery is that which will be revealed to those who love God (1 Cor. 2.9–10).

When we delve into the depths of Scripture, as we have already touched on briefly, we discover that it has much to tell us about God's oneness. We encounter prayers, such as that in Ephesians, that God 'may grant that you may be strengthened in your inner being with power through his Spirit, and that Christ may dwell in your hearts through faith, as you are being rooted and grounded in love' so that 'you may have the power to comprehend, with all the saints, what is the breadth and length and height and depth, and to know the love of Christ that surpasses knowledge' (Eph. 3.16–19).

The doctrine of the Trinity may be complex and mysterious, but – as the passages from Matthew and 2 Corinthians made clear – it is never conceived as an abstract reality. Rather, the Trinity is a tangible and present reality in our lives, community, relationships and sacraments. The three persons of the Trinity are not united in theory. They are eternally united with one another in love, a love that is poured out endlessly between the Father, Son and Spirit who are completely equal – and yet possess a unique dignity and identity. And as persons created in God's image, able to know and love God and one another, the Trinity describes the relationship we are called to have with one another and with all of creation in its most perfect form. The Trinity is the perfect form of community and, as we discover in Chapter 3, the perfect description of divine joy.

Through the foundation of the Trinity, therefore, God is revealed to those who love God through the Spirit who searches everything. In other words, the mystery of God is revealed as we encounter God in prayer, in relationship, and ultimately in sacrament. Through the foundation of the Trinity we are able to pray, for it is the Son and the Spirit who intercede for us to God, and the Spirit who bears witness with our spirit (Rom. 8.16). Through the foundation of the Trinity we proclaim Christ as Lord, for we are told that 'no one can say "Jesus is Lord" except by the Holy Spirit' (1 Cor. 12.3). Through the Trinity, we claim our identity as children of God as God sends the Spirit into our hearts, enabling us to cry out to God as newly adopted children of our Father (Gal. 4.6). And God as Father, Son and Spirit is most tangibly encountered through the sacraments of baptism and the Eucharist.

Baptism, as Chapter 9 of this book makes clear, is one of the sacraments given to us by Christ, who was baptized. At Christ's baptism, the Father speaks and affirms that this is 'my beloved Son' (e.g. Matt. 1.17); the Son is baptized, and the Holy Spirit descends upon him. The whole Trinity is present at the Jordan to reveal this mystery. Such a connection between the Trinity and baptism is also clear in the final command of Jesus to his disciples, that they are to go out into the world and to baptize in the name of the Father, Son and Spirit (Matt. 28.19).

Furthermore, God as Father, Son and Spirit is tangibly encountered in the sacrament of the Eucharist, also given to us by Christ. In this great sacrament we address God as Father, we pray the words the Son gave us on the night before he died, and we invoke the power of the Holy Spirit. And in this great sacrament, we then receive the presence of God's Son, through the power of the Holy Spirit, as the gracious gift of the Father. Through the foundation of the Trinity, we become participants in the divine love and life that God as Father, Son and Holy Spirit share. Rather than just a mysterious doctrine or concept that makes no sense, the Trinity is the lens through which our Christian lives *do* make sense. The Trinity shows us how to live and love and imitate God in Christ with the love poured into our very being by and through the Spirit.

The Trinity teaches us about relationship. Certainly, God is one and there is only one God. But God the Father is not the Father without the Son, because a son cannot be a son without a father. In the New Testament, God is unequivocally 'the God and Father of our Lord Jesus Christ' (Eph. 1.3; 2 Cor. 11.31) and Jesus is unequivocally the 'Son' who 'did not regard equality with God as something to be exploited' (Phil. 2.6). God is absolutely essential to Jesus' identity and Jesus is absolutely essential to God's. God's identity is established by God's relation to Christ and Christ's identity is established by his relation to God. And the Spirit is an integral part of this relationship, not simply a later add-on, because the Spirit is known not only as the Holy Spirit throughout the New Testament, but is also named interchangeably as 'the Spirit of God' (1 Cor. 2.11) and 'the Spirit of Christ' (Phil. 1.19). As such, in the familiar text from 2 Corinthians mentioned at the start of this chapter concerning the love of God, the grace of Christ, and the community of the Holy Spirit, we come to see that knowing God's love, Christ's grace, and the community of the Spirit cannot be separated from the God who loves, the Christ who gives grace, and the Spirit who searches all things.

God the Holy Trinity, therefore, is about more than knowledge and comprehension of a mystery. Certainly knowledge is important for understanding the connection between Father, Son and Spirit. We find in John's Gospel, for instance, the words of Jesus to his followers that 'if you know me, you will know my Father also' (John 14.7). Jesus' prayer to the Father later in the same Gospel makes a similar claim, 'that they may know you, the only true God, and Jesus Christ whom you have sent' (John 17.3). As Jesus promises his disciples that he will not leave them comfortless but will send the Holy Spirit, the Comforter, to dwell with and in them, he reminds them time and again that by knowing him and seeing him, they know and see the Father. Through the Son, the invisible God is made visible. Through the Son, the unknowable God is made known. Through the Son, the incomprehensible love of God is made tangible.

When it comes to knowing God as Father, Son and Spirit, it is ultimately through love that we comprehend this great mystery. This is the love whereby God acts and gives God's very self for us in the suffering and death of Christ and in the gift of the Holy Spirit. Only because God is Father, Son and Spirit can God love and know us in the way that God does. Knowledge of God in Christ and in the Spirit is central to how we understand the Trinity, but it is through love that the Trinity is truly known. As we will discover in Chapter 10 on Scripture, the language of love is woven into the fabric of the Bible. Love is also woven into the very fabric of the Trinity. Ultimately, therefore, it is not the Trinity that makes no sense but the love through which God knows us and by which God is known.

For this love is not the kind of love we imagine or relate to our own experience of love. This love is not self-centred and self-absorbed. This love is not the kind of love that leads us to feel separate from the world, floating above reality, disconnected from the mess of our lives. Rather, this is a love that calls us into the world, into deeper relationship with all of God's creation. This is a love that cannot be contained in a focus on one person, but that pours out from the dynamic relationship of three in one.

So we read Jesus' promise in John's Gospel that 'As the Father has loved me, so I have loved you; abide in my love … This is my commandment, that you love one another as I have loved you' (John 15.9, 12). John is clear about the connection made through love between Father and Son and the demands placed on us to love as we are loved. The connection to the Spirit is then brought home in the words not only of John's Gospel, but of the apostle Paul who tells us that this love, God's love 'has been poured into our hearts through the Holy Spirit' (Rom. 5.5).

Love thus achieves what knowledge cannot. This is perhaps most clear in the words often found at the centre of a wedding service: those of 1 Corinthians 13. This well-known text begins with the clarification by Paul that: 'If I speak in the tongues of mortals and of angels, but do not have love, I am a noisy gong or a clanging cymbal. And if I have prophetic powers, and understand all mysteries and all knowledge, and if I have all faith, so as to remove mountains, but do not have love, I am nothing' (1 Cor. 13.1–2). Without love, our knowledge and words are simply noise, our understanding even of 'all mysteries' is nought, and what we possess is worthless.

This love we are called to give, the love we are called to share with our world, stems directly from the love of God in Christ Jesus our Lord from which we cannot be separated, and that has been poured into our hearts through the Spirit. At the heart of the Trinity, at the heart of our understanding of God as three in one, is love, which is the essence of the relationship between Father, Son and Spirit. And while the doctrine of the Trinity may be connected to theological controversy and Church councils, ultimately the roots of God as three in one are found in encounters with God in Scripture, in sacrament, in prayer, and in relationship.

This is perhaps most clear when Paul tells us in Romans that 'we know that all things work together for good for those who love God, who are called according to his purpose' (Rom. 8.28). For, struggle as we might to comprehend that which makes no sense, and challenging as it is at times to love God and those around us, Paul is clear in language that draws us back to the Trinity that: 'the Spirit helps us in our weakness; for we do not know how to pray as we ought, but that very Spirit intercedes with sighs too deep for words. And God, who searches the heart, knows what is the mind of the Spirit, because the Spirit intercedes for the saints according to the will of God' (Rom. 8.26–27). And it is not only the Spirit who intercedes for us, but also 'Christ Jesus, who died, yes, who was raised, who is at the right hand of God, who indeed intercedes for us' so that absolutely nothing can 'separate us from the love of God in Christ Jesus our Lord' (Rom. 8.34,39).

Our belief in God who is three in one has direct consequences for our lives. The Trinity challenges us not to fear mystery and not to back away from the challenges of community, justice and upholding the equality and dignity of all. Embracing the mystery of God, Christians are sent by the Spirit to bear witness to the good news of Christ for the sake of the world God created and loves. God's love for us and our love for one another cannot be detached and are forever united in the Trinity. Thus, the deepest mystery of the Trinity is not how it is that God is one as Father, Son and Spirit, but how this dynamic relationship and outpouring of love is the foundation for the entire Christian life. For, as one of the authors of this book made clear in a recent sermon, 'an act of love is an act of God, and the true act of God, the true act of love, is something which our own failures and weaknesses and selfishness can never diminish' (Groves, 2018). In the economy of God, nothing is wasted.

When we think about loving God who is Father, Son and Spirit, just as the relationship between the persons of the Trinity is not static, neither is the one we have with this God. Ultimately, knowing and loving God as Father, Son and Spirit are not one and the same. Rather, we love God not because we know God, but because God knows us. The foundation for the love of God is God already knowing the one who loves and God already calling the one who loves. God is the one who pours love into our hearts through the Spirit. God is the one in whom, and Christ is the one through whom, we exist. For the love of God comes directly from the 'one God, the Father, from whom are all things and for whom we exist, and one Lord, Jesus Christ, through whom are all things and through whom we exist' (1 Cor. 8.6). The relationship between

Father and Son is not only the foundation for how we understand God as Trinity, but it is also the foundation for how we love this same God.

This foundation of love, however, is continually challenged by the reality that despite our best efforts, the love we give remains at times self-absorbed. The hope we find in God as Trinity comes from the reality of the Holy Spirit who sighs and intercedes to God for us. For such deep sighing and such intercession for us and for all creation point to the reality that these actions can only come from those who have seen the hope of salvation, but have not fully grasped it. Those who know God's promise, those who know God's love in Christ through the Spirit, sigh for its completion and fulfilment. The reality that only the Spirit and only Christ can fully know and intercede for us with God, combined with God's love for us and our love of God, moves us with faith to embrace the hope of salvation. This is a hope that, in a way that brings us back full circle to Romans, cannot disappoint those whose hearts have had God's love poured into them through the Spirit.

Further Reading

Collins, Paul M. (2008), *The Trinity: A Guide for the Perplexed*, London: Continuum.

Emery, Gilles OP and Levering, Matthew (eds) (2011), *The Oxford Handbook of the Trinity*, New York: Oxford University Press.

Tanner, Kathryn (2001), *Jesus, Humanity and the Trinity: A Brief Systematic Theology*, Edinburgh: T & T Clark.

Westhaver, George (2018), *A Transforming Vision: Knowing and Loving the Triune God*, London: SCM Press.

3

Love Overflowing – The Doctrine of Creation

Jonathan Jong

Creation myths

Once upon a time before time, there was an egg and, in it, Yin and Yang were in chaos. P'an Ku was also in the egg, sleeping for 18,000 years. When he awoke, he pushed up with his hands and down with his feet, and the egg broke asunder, and Yang became the heavens and Yin became the earth. Another 18,000 years passed, and as P'an Ku grew and grew, so too did the heavens and the earth grow farther and farther apart. When P'an Ku died, his body gave the world its form: his flesh became fertile land and his bones precious minerals, his left eye became the Sun and his right eye the Moon, his sweat became rain, and his breath the winds and mists and clouds, his fur became forests and his beard stars.

Or, Ranginui and Papatūānuku held each other in tight embrace, and their children were born in the darkness between them, and there they had to dwell. The fierce Tūmatauenga suggested to his brothers that they slay their parents to escape from this stifling embrace, but the peaceful Tāne-mahuta disagreed, saying that they should instead push their father and mother apart. And so they did, and thus the gods were freed, each to exercise their powers in the new world, over seas and winds, trees and crops, birds and reptiles. Tāne also dressed his father, with the stars and the Moon and Sun. To this day, Ranginui and Papatūānuku yearn for each other: Ranginui's tears fall upon his beloved Papatūānuku as rain, and her sighs rise up as mist from the forest and her strains to reach him cause all things to quake.

Or, Aslan sang in the darkness and brought forth from it a thousand thousand stars, each with their own voices to join the Lion's song. As he sang, the eastern sky turned from black to grey to white to pink to gold, and the air shook and shook until the young Sun arose, revealing hills and valleys and rivers, still naked in their newness, from which life was to spring. And so it did, as Aslan walked about: the grass sprouted forth and spread from him like waves, and trees as well. Before long, the Lion changed his tune again, and this time the earth bubbled and burst and from each crumbling mound emerged creatures large and small, dogs and deer, butterflies and elephants, beavers and frogs. 'Narnia, Narnia, Narnia, awake,' said Aslan, 'Love. Think. Speak. Be walking trees. Be talking beasts. Be divine waters.'

Creation stories – like these from China, Aotearoa New Zealand, and C. S. Lewis's novel *The Magician's Nephew* from his Chronicles of Narnia series – can be found all over the world. Hundreds have been recorded and collected and analysed by anthropologists working among diverse cultures on every continent. There is scholarly debate over what such stories mean, and how and why they have been told and retold, but we can be certain that there is more to them than straightforwardly literal readings would suggest. Creation myths may well be attempts to explain the origins of the world, but they also carry moral, political and ritual significance for the communities that tell them. The stories found in the Bible are no exception.

The Bible contains multiple narratives and images about the creation of the world. Most people are familiar with the two main creation myths at the beginning of the book of Genesis, but there are more besides, tucked away in the Psalms, in the book of Job, and elsewhere. In Genesis 1, the world begins as a dark and formless void, comprising mostly water. Creation looks easy here. God speaks, and it is so; light and land and sun and stars and birds and beasts all come into being at God's whim and word. In six days, God makes the world, finishing it off with human beings – 'male and female he created them' (Gen. 1.27) – and, on the seventh day, God rested. The end of this first account emphasizes that the seventh day is hallowed, which reminds readers of the commandment to rest on the Sabbath (Exod. 20.8–11).

Genesis 2 tells quite a different story, in which God makes things as an artisan might. The story here begins with God forming a man out of dust and breathing life into him. Before a single drop of rain had fallen, before plants and herbs had begun to grow, before any other living creatures were made, God made a man, and then a garden for him to make a home. God also makes a woman, but this comes later, after no suitable partner for the man could be found among the other animals that God had made. Here, at the end of the second account, the reader is told that 'therefore a man leaves his father and his mother and clings to his wife, and they become one flesh' (Gen. 2.24); thus a straight line is drawn from the creation myth to marriage practices.

Besides these clear connections to the Sabbath and marriage

respectively, the creation accounts in Genesis have also been received by Jews and Christians as carrying ethical implications concerning human reproduction and our use and care of the natural environment, particularly from God's command to 'be fruitful and multiply, and fill the earth and subdue it; and have dominion' (Gen. 1.28). All of this is to say that the meaning and significance of creation myths go far beyond their literal senses: indeed, the fact that there are these two different accounts in Genesis 1 and 2 is a clue that to focus on the literal descriptions is to miss the point altogether.

The broader significance of creation myths can also be seen in the other, more fleeting, pictures of creation in the psalmody and poetry of the Hebrew Bible, in which the themes of creation and salvation are often intertwined. For example, Psalm 74 is a plea to God to save the nation, which draws on images of God ordering the world by subduing forces of chaos:

> Yet God my King is from of old, working salvation in the earth. You divided the sea by your might; you broke the heads of the dragons in the waters. You crushed the heads of Leviathan; you gave him as food for the creatures of the wilderness. You cut openings for springs and torrents; you dried up ever-flowing streams. Yours is the day, yours also the night; you established the luminaries and the sun. You have fixed all the bounds of the earth; you made summer and winter. (Ps. 74.12–17)

This image of God triumphing over water and its monstrous inhabitants appears throughout Scripture (Isa. 51; Ps. 89; Job 9) and is even echoed in Genesis 1, which describes water in the darkness before God's first creative act that brings light to the world. The subjugation of water brings creation and the exodus

– especially the miraculous parting of the Red Sea – together, as can be seen in Isaiah 51: 'Was it not you who cut Rahab in pieces, who pierced the dragon? Was it not you who dried up the sea, the waters of the great deep; who made the depths of the sea a way for the redeemed to cross over?' (Isa. 51.9–10).

This theme of creation out of watery chaos also appears in other ancient Near Eastern cultures, such as in the Babylonian creation myth *Enuma Elish*, composed well over 3,000 years ago. In *Enuma Elish*, the earth and skies are made by the wind god Marduk out of the body of the god of the ocean, Tiamat, whom he killed in battle. Some scholars have suggested that Genesis 1 was written partly in response to these polytheistic ideas that divinize different aspects of the natural world: in contrast, Genesis 1 describes a God who calls forth creation from the dark waters simply by speaking, without even the need to struggle against chaotic forces. If so, then this creation myth serves yet another purpose, that of differentiating the God of the ancient Israelites from the gods of neighbouring cultures.

Creation out of nothing

We have just seen that the Bible contains images of God speaking into a watery void and fashioning things out of clay and battling sea monsters, but Christians generally do not believe that God is in possession of vocal cords or hands or limbs, with which to speak or sculpt or wrestle. These descriptions must therefore be metaphorical. Indeed, Christians usually emphasize that, for God, creation is totally effortless. Even the idea that God creates by speaking is really a way of expressing this idea that God does not have to do anything to create the world: God simply commands the world into existence, wills all things into being. Christians also emphasize that God creates the world out of nothing. Unlike P'an Ku or the children of Ranginui and Papatūānuku, God does not craft the world out of pre-existing matter, neither broken eggshells nor the bodies of parental gods nor anything else. When Christians say that they believe that God created the world 'out of nothing', they are certainly not saying that nothingness is a kind of stuff out of which the world is made. Rather, Christians are simply denying that God makes the world out of anything at all. Or, put in positive terms, Christians affirm that God made *everything*, such that were it not for God's creative activity, there would exist nothing at all.

It is quite unimaginable, this business of God creating out of nothing. This is because it is psychologically impossible to imagine true nothingness. At best, we can imagine a dark space, which is then filled with things, like in the story C. S. Lewis tells about Aslan singing in the darkness or, for that matter, the story in Genesis 1 about God speaking into the void. But a dark space about which we can speak of an empty prior state is itself a thing, and Christians want to insist that God is the creator of *all* things, including empty space and even time. But why do we insist on this idea, as difficult as it is to imagine? It is because the Christian doctrine of creation is really a part of the Christian doctrine of God, no less than the doctrine of the Trinity is. How we talk about creation says something important about what we believe about God. The doctrine of creation out of nothing says two related things about God. First, it draws a fundamental and absolute distinction between God and *everything*. If God created all things, then God cannot be a thing, cannot be counted among objects in the complete catalogue of all existent things that might include humans and humpback whales, quarks and quinoa, numbers and Norway. Some people refer to this as God's *transcendence* over creation. Second, the Christian doctrine of creation posits a fundamental and absolute asymmetry between God and everything: everything depends on God for its existence, and God depends on nothing whatsoever, being entirely self-sufficient (or self-subsistent, as theologians say). Some people – admittedly, very few people – refer to this asymmetry as God's *aseity* (from Latin *a* 'from' and *se* 'self').

Divine transcendence should not be confused with the idea that God is very, very powerful; more powerful than our feeble minds can comprehend. To say that God is more powerful than us assumes that God and creatures can be compared on the same scale, though the scale is bound to be very long, perhaps going from zero to infinity. But infinity is not a number, and the Christian assertion that God is infinite is not to say that very, very large numbers apply to God: it is, rather, to say that God is beyond quantification altogether. God and creatures are not to be compared, not because it is very difficult to do so, but because such a comparison makes no sense. To compare things, they have to have something in common. For example, to compare the weight of two things, they both have to be the kinds of things that have mass: it makes very little sense to compare the weights of a watermelon and the number seven. It would not even really be right to say that the watermelon is heavier than the number seven because abstract entities weigh nothing: the number seven is simply not the kind of thing for which mass is a relevant property. It makes even less sense – no sense at all – to compare God and creatures, because God is not a thing of any kind, and therefore shares no properties with any things.

The idea that God is self-sufficient, without dependence on anything other than God, turns out to be a surprisingly rich idea. It leads, for example, to the idea that God is *simple*, which sounds like an insult, but just means that God does not consist of parts. God must be simple, because if God consisted of parts, God's existence would depend on the existence of those parts: but God's existence does not depend on anything, so God cannot consist of parts. The doctrine of divine simplicity, in turn, leads to the idea that God cannot change. When something changes, it is really its parts that change. If they were to change totally, we would say that they were no longer themselves. For example, when we observe a change in a person, we are observing a change in some aspect of them: their weight, their hair colour, their beliefs and preferences. If, on the other hand, we observed a person turning into a pumpkin, it would be more accurate to say that the person no longer really existed, and that a pumpkin had replaced them. Since God consists of no parts, it follows that God also consists of no *changeable* parts, so God cannot change. Or, at least, God does not change in any way that we can understand, given that our understanding of change comes from our observation of created things.

These may seem like abstruse philosophical points, even less interesting than the idea with which we began, that God creates everything out of nothing. And yet, Christian theologians have insisted on this absolute difference between God and creatures since they first began thinking and writing about God as creator. Indeed, the alternative view, that God is a very powerful person or force – like us in some ways, but greater in every way – has not only been considered to be mistaken, but (as we will see in Chapter 5 on the incarnation) idolatrous. This is because God's transcendence, aseity, simplicity and changelessness (or immutability, as some people say) are important for how we think about lots of other things, including even the meaning and value of life itself.

Creation for no reason

Humans make things. We make art and crafts and tools and products and children. We make things for many reasons, and benefit from the things we make in various ways. We make tools to make practical tasks easier. We manufacture products for trade. We might make art and poetry to fulfil our need to express our-selves, or to challenge prevailing cultural mores, or for fame and fortune. If we are honest with ourselves, perhaps we even have children in part because they give a sense of meaning and purpose to our lives, and obtain for us a sort of symbolic immortality. As valuable as some human creative activities are for helping us think about God, none of these reasons for our creating apply to God and God's creating of the world. The world and its contents – including human beings – do not exist to benefit God in any way at all, do not exist to fulfil any need in God. God, being self-sufficient, has no needs to fulfil. God, being changeless, cannot even really be affected by creatures, as effects imply change: there is not even the possibility of God gaining any benefit from us.

Creation is useless. We are useless to God. It is a glorious thing indeed to be useless, because it means that our value is not de-pendent on our utility. We may be accustomed to talking about 'natural resources' or, worse still, 'human resources', but the Christian doctrine of creation is a repudiation of this view of things and people. The world is not, for God, a resource to be used; we are not the means of production, or means to any end at all. It might make us feel good to think that we make God happy, but this is really just a form of self-flattery. The Presbyterian *Westminster Shorter Catechism* famously states that 'Man's chief end is to glorify God, and to enjoy him forever' (Westminster Assembly, 1986, Question 1), which is easily and often misinterpreted as suggesting that God made human beings to massage the divine ego. It is as if God needed our devotion and affection to feel loved and happy. Nothing could be further from the truth. Setting aside for a moment that divine happiness can be nothing like our happiness, which is mediated by brain function and fluctuates with the ebbs and flows of our fortune, God is in any case *perfectly* happy: the life of the Trinity is the eternal delight of love outpoured between the Father, the Son and the Spirit. There is nothing that anything or anyone could possibly add to the divine joy.

Quite contrary to the idea that we are made in order for God to feel loved, the love of God for us is the basis of our existence. This is not to say that God made us to have something to love, which is what people sometimes say about why they want to have children or pets. God has neither need for love, nor need to express love: God has no needs of any kind. Nevertheless, everything that exists does so because God loves it into being. This is admittedly an odd way of talking. When we love something, it first has to exist (or else we only love the idea of the thing, and ideas exist in the mind); only then can we decide to love it, or find ourselves compelled to love it. The Christian doctrine of creation denies that this applies to God: the love of God for the world is not God's evaluative reaction to a thing that God has made or imagined. God's love is not conditioned upon how the world happened to have turned out, though it is easy to make this mistake from the refrain in Genesis 1 that 'God saw that it was good'.

To say that God loved the world into being is just to say that creation is the result of the love of God outpoured, just as the life of the Trinity consists in the pouring out of love between Father, Son and Spirit (as we discovered more fully in Chapter 2). Thus, the doctrine of creation and the doctrine of the Trinity are connected: God's creative act is an expression of God's nature, as creation is the overflow of the love that the Father, Son and Spirit share. There is, of course, nothing into which this love can be poured, not even empty space: and so love makes love's recipient, the cosmos, and all that is in it. And just as the sharing of love within the life of the Trinity is an act and not an accident, so creation is not the accidental spillage of surplus love, but the manifestation of God's exuberant willingness to '[call] into existence the things that do not exist' (Rom. 4.17). This is to say that God did not need to create anything at all, but did, out of boundless love. The chief end of creation, then, is indeed to glorify and enjoy God, but this is true because God glories in our enjoyment of this love that creates and sustains and saves us.

The integrity of created things

The idea that our value does not primarily rest in our productivity or ingenuity or physical prowess might sit uneasily in our minds, formed as they are in individualistic and meritocratic societies that prize such things. Having been taught that self-reliance is our only security in a competitive world, we might be anxious about the idea that we – not only our value, but our very existence – depend wholly on God. However, far from robbing us of our own value, the fact that creation is the utterly gratuitous act of God, without even the possibility of reciprocation, is precisely what guarantees us against devaluation by market forces or rumour mills or neurochemical imbalances. No one can make us anything less than what we are, not even ourselves. Or, as Paul puts it, 'neither death, nor life, nor angels, nor rulers, nor things present, nor things to come, nor powers, nor height, nor depth, nor anything else in all creation, will be able to separate us from the love of God in Christ Jesus our Lord' (Rom. 8.38–39).

Just as our value is a pure gift, so is our freedom and integrity. The idea that God is the ultimate source of everything sometimes triggers worries that we are no more than marionettes in a cosmic stage production or pieces moved by the divine chess master. In other words, we are powerless but to bend at the irresistible will of an omnipotent tyrant-god. The assumption that underlies this anxiety seems to be that power between God and creation is a zero-sum game, such that the more power we ascribe to God, the less there is for us. This puts God and creatures in a competitive relationship. But just as there can be no comparison between God and creatures, so there can be no competition between God and creatures either. Competition, like comparison, requires at least some degree of similarity – tennis players compete with one another for Grand Slams, as do plants for sunlight, and commercial enterprises for market share, and scientific theories for variance explained – but the difference between God and creatures is absolute: there is no category that contains both. Far from being an impediment to our integrity and freedom, God provides as a gift the conditions for integrity and freedom, without whom we would not just lack integrity and freedom, but even existence itself.

Speaking of scientific theories, it might now be easier to see why no scientific theory about the origins of the universe could possibly contradict – or, for that matter, provide evidence for – the Christian doctrine of creation. This is because unlike creation *myths*, which are at least superficially about the early chronology of the universe, the Christian *doctrine* of creation is unconcerned with such things. In fact, even if the universe had no beginning at all – if it had always existed – our doctrine of creation would remain the same: God would still be the source of all things, who freely and gratuitously donates existence to the world, and without whose creative activity nothing whatsoever would exist. The relevant fact about the universe for the doctrine of creation is not that it began however many billions of years ago, but that it exists at all. There is nothing necessary about the world's existence – it could just as easily not have existed, though this is as difficult to imagine as sheer nothingness is; and the fact that it does exist is the thing that is theologically interesting.

This *contingency* of and in the universe is, incidentally, also what makes science interesting. Scientists cannot infer facts about the world from logic alone or from first philosophical principles. The idea, found in Plato's *Timaeus* that the universe should be spherical in shape because the sphere 'of all shapes is the most perfect and the most self-similar' (Plato, *Timaeus*, 1929, 33b) makes little sense to scientists, who insist on going out into the world to observe what it is like through cautious observation and experiment. When they do so, they find that the answer to their questions is often 'It depends'. At what temperature does water boil? It depends on the atmospheric pressure of where the boiling happens. How quickly will a bacterial population evolve? It depends on the rate of mutation and strength of selection pressures, including the use and abuse of antibiotics by human beings. How long will a human being live? It depends on the availability of food, shelter and medicine, and exposure to disease, accident and violence, and a myriad of other factors. Objects in the world, scientists tell us, exist in complex relationships of interdependence. The world in its entirety, say Christians, exists in a relationship of utter dependence upon God.

It is not just that the beginnings of the universe fall outside the purview of the doctrine of creation. What Christians believe about God – that God is transcendent and self-sufficient – also means that it makes no sense to pit theology against science. For the doctrine of creation to be in competition with a scientific theory, they both have to be positing competing causal factors. For example, when we ask 'Who broke the vase? Peter or John?', what we have are two candidates – Peter and John – who are both similar kinds of 'things'. This is still true if Peter was (as you might expect) a little boy and John was a kitten or even a hurricane. Regardless, Peter and John are both objects in the physical world, and this commonality between them allows them to be rival explanatory candidates. As Christians – and this chapter – have insisted, God's transcendence makes comparison and competition of this kind nonsensical.

Even if we are not tempted to pit the doctrine of creation against the big bang theory (which, by the way, is credited to a Roman Catholic priest, Georges Lemaître), we might be tempted to include God in the timeline of the early expansion of the universe. We imagine that God started the big bang – just as I might start a fire by lighting a match – and then a hot and dense singularity expands so rapidly that the laws of nature as we know them may not apply to the first picosecond (10^{-12} seconds) of the process, and then just about 10^{-6} seconds later the first protons and neutrons form, and so forth, until you are reading this book. So, God is the first in a series of causes, like a billiard player who moves their hand to adjust the stick that strikes the cue ball that hits another ball that drops into the pot. But this will not do, because – divine transcendence is relevant here too – not being an object alongside other objects, God is not a cause among causes. This basic idea extends beyond what we make of the big bang theory to how we think about science more generally, including such topics of modern controversy as the theory of evolution by natural selection or psychological theories about religion. 'God did it' is never a competing explanation to the theories scientists construct and test by observation and experiment. Rather, God has gifted to the world – along with existence itself, and value – also its own causal integrity: by the grace of God, we creatures are real causes in the world, and it is these creaturely causes that intrigue natural and social scientists. God, meanwhile, is always and everywhere, in every fermion and boson, and neurone and hormone, and star and nebula in the still expanding universe, freely donating existence to the whole thing, keeping it going for as long as it goes.

This, then, is what it means to be a creature: to have our origins in God who cannot but love and love without condition and without remain; to always be held in existence in the creative love of God; and to be free to give love to others just as we receive love ourselves.

Further Reading

Johnson, Elizabeth A. (2015), *Ask the Beasts: Darwin and the God of Love*, London: Bloomsbury.

Lash, Nicholas (2004), *Holiness, Speech, and Silence. Reflections on the Question of God*, Aldershot, UK: Ashgate.

McCabe, Herbert (2013), 'God and Creation', *New Blackfriars*, 94 (1052), pp. 385–95.

Oliver, Simon (2017), *Creation: A Guide for the Perplexed*, London: Bloomsbury.

Williams, Rowan (1999), 'On Being Creatures' in *On Christian Theology*, Oxford: Wiley, pp. 63–78.

4

Love Realized – The Spirit of Life

Judith M. Brown

The Holy Spirit: love neglected?

The Holy Spirit is often wrongly thought to be the poor relation of Christian theology. Even within the Church, the Spirit hardly seems to be at the front and centre of our preaching and our worship. The great Christian Feast of Pentecost, which remembers and celebrates the gift of the Holy Spirit to the first disciples after Christ's resurrection and ascension (Acts 2), is one of the most important festivals of the Church's year, but those outside the Church would seldom notice. This is partly because Pentecost is almost impossible to commercialize: no chance of cribs and angels, parties and presents, or eggs and hares, in the way that the wider society has taken hold of Christmas and Easter. Pentecost celebrates the gift of God's Spirit that is poured into the hearts of those who love and seek to follow Christ. So, rather than being neglected by the Church, the Spirit is that which is presupposed by all that we do as Christians. It is the breathing that we do not notice but without which we would expire. The Spirit is the gift that empowers Christians to live the Christian life. By the power of the Holy Spirit the Church itself comes into being.

When new Christians are welcomed into the Church through the sacrament of baptism (see Chapter 9), they receive the same Spirit that we encounter right at the beginning of the stories of Jesus. All the Gospel writers begin their account of Jesus' ministry with the assertion that God's Spirit descended on him. The Gospel of Mark testifies that Jesus was baptized in the River Jordan by his cousin John, and 'just as he was coming up out of the water, he saw the heavens torn apart and the Spirit descending like a dove on him. And a voice came from heaven, "You are my Son, the Beloved; with you I am well pleased" ' (Mark 1.10–11). The Holy Spirit was the source of Jesus' ministry that drove and empowered him and animated his preaching. Luke describes Jesus as consciously appropriating the words of the prophet Isaiah, that in the fullness of time God's chosen servant, anointed with the Spirit, would bring redemption to God's people. In Luke 4, Jesus stands up in the synagogue of his home town of Nazareth and reads aloud this passage from Isaiah that tells of the Spirit of the Lord being upon his servant to bring good news to the poor, freedom for prisoners and sight to the blind. Amazingly, as he gave back the reading to the attendant Jesus told the congregation that on that very day this Scripture had been fulfilled in their hearing (Luke 4.16–21; see also Isa. 61.1–2).

This fulfilment points us to the gift of the same Spirit that Jesus promised to his disciples before his crucifixion as he prepared them not just for his violent death, but also for the new life that would transform and empower them. As John's Gospel reminds us, Jesus was filled with an urgent compassion for his closest followers in their last hours together. Gathered with his disciples, Jesus promises his Spirit as his continued presence among them:

'I will ask the Father, and he will give you another Advocate, to be with you for ever. This is the Spirit of truth, whom the world cannot receive, because it neither sees him nor knows him. You know him, because he abides with you, and he will be in you. I will not leave you orphaned; I am coming to you' (John 14.5–18).

John's Gospel later describes how the grief-stricken Mary Magdalen meets the risen Christ in the garden where his body was laid in a new tomb. She mistakes him for the gardener but, when he speaks her name, she recognizes him and longs to embrace and hold on to him. But Jesus gently tells her not to hold on to him as he has not yet ascended to the Father. Jesus says this because – as we will see in Chapter 8 – through his resurrection and ascension he will be present with, and in, his friends in a more intimate and powerful way than would ever have been possible had he remained. So Jesus comforts his disciples who long for his presence with the promise of the Spirit and is clear that: 'Those who love me will keep my word, and my Father will love them, and we will come to them and make our home with them' (John 14.23).

The Holy Spirit in the Old Testament

The earliest Jewish Christians who heard the stories of Christ and later read the accounts of Pentecost in the Acts of the Apostles would have been very familiar with the idea of God's Spirit working in the world and moving among people from the Jewish Scriptures. The great narrative of creation in Genesis 1 – discussed in depth in the previous chapter – depicts the Spirit of God as the force of creation and new life. God's Spirit in the form of wind (spirit and wind are the same word in Hebrew) swept across the great void out of which light and dark, sea, sky, land, and all that lives on land, were created. In the Old Testament the Spirit of God is also a constant, divine force in the world, creating and re-creating humankind and the natural order. Numerous leaders and prophets are empowered and inspired by the Spirit, particularly Moses and King David. Elsewhere in the Old Testament, the prophet Ezekiel had a vision of a valley full of dry bones that were raised and transformed into a vast multitude of living people by the Spirit or breath of God. These represented the people of Israel to whom God spoke through his prophet: 'And you shall know that I am the LORD, when I open your graves, and bring you up from your graves, O my people. I will put my spirit within you, and you shall live ...' (Ezek. 37.13–14). The prophet Joel also spoke of the Spirit of God, which would be poured out on all men and women, even slaves, and would give power and insight to them. In Joel 2, God promises that: 'I will pour out my spirit on all flesh; your sons and your daughters shall prophesy, your old men shall dream dreams, and your young men shall see visions. Even on the male and female slaves, in those days, I will pour out my spirit' (Joel 2.28–29). And of course, in the passage from Isaiah, quoted by Jesus in the Nazareth synagogue, there was a belief that God's messianic servant would be anointed and empowered by the Spirit.

This was the religious context in which Jesus taught, where belief about an active Spirit of God was already present in the minds of many of his followers through their knowledge of Jewish Scripture. Such a context explains Jesus' reaction to the Jewish religious leader Nicodemus, who came to see him secretly at night and seemed unable to grasp Jesus' teaching that those who hoped to see the kingdom of God would have to be born again by the Spirit. Jesus asked him how he, a teacher of Israel and therefore one who knew the texts about the presence of the Spirit described above, did not understand this (John 3.1–10). Given this background to the experience of the disciples at Pentecost, it is not surprising that the Spirit is described as experiencing a mighty wind – the same wind or spirit that brought creation into being, that brought to life the dry bones of Ezekiel's vision, that God had promised to pour out on all people. Furthermore, the book of Acts also describes this experience of the Spirit with the imagery of tongues of fire (Acts 2.2–3). Once again, this is an image of the divine presence that stretches deep into Jewish religious understanding. Moses encountered God in fire – in a bush that burned but was not destroyed. Further, when the children of Israel had fled from Egypt they experienced the presence of God as a fire by night and a cloud by day to guide and protect them. And when the prophet Malachi spoke of the messenger who would prepare the way of the Lord, he describes the presence of this divine messenger as one who is 'like a refiner's fire' (Mal. 3.2).

The Holy Spirit in the New Testament

The reality, the presence, of the Holy Spirit is also everywhere and palpable in the New Testament. As mentioned above, for the earliest Christians the presence and work of the Spirit was the way they experienced, in their lives and within their communities, the ongoing presence of the risen Christ. It was impossible to be a Christian without the indwelling and enabling Spirit. When the apostles in Jerusalem heard that many in the city of Samaria had turned to faith in Christ and had been baptized, they sent Peter and John to them. We are told in Acts that 'The two went down and prayed for them that they might receive the Holy Spirit (for as yet the Spirit had not come upon any of them; they had only been baptized in the name of the Lord Jesus). Then Peter and John laid their hands on them, and they received the Holy Spirit' (Acts 8.15–17).

This story of Peter and John, though, is not the only time such a reception of the Spirit occurs. The language of giving and receiving the Holy Spirit is spread across the story of the early Church in the book of Acts. In Acts 10, the gift of the Holy Spirit to Gentiles (those who are not Jewish), just as to the first Jewish Christians, convinced Peter that Gentiles too should be baptized. How could they not baptize those who had received the Spirit, just as the first disciples had done? Even later, in Acts 19, Paul arrives in Ephesus, finds some disciples, and immediately asks them if they have received the Holy Spirit. With disarming honesty they replied that they had never heard of the Holy Spirit! It transpired that they had received the same sort of baptism for repentance that John the Baptist had been preaching before the ministry of Jesus. So Paul ensures they are now baptized in the name of Jesus, and he laid his hands on them and they received the Holy Spirit. Importantly, we see here not only the connection between the early Church and the movement of the Spirit, but also the tangible connection between baptism and the reception of the Holy Spirit.

The book of Acts does not just show that the gift of the Spirit was essential to being a Christian disciple. It records how the early Christians actually experienced the Spirit not as an impersonal general force, but as one who was deeply personal. By the Spirit they were enabled to speak to large crowds, sometimes in languages they did not themselves know. In what some call speaking in 'tongues', early Christians could communicate with people from other parts of the world. They found the courage to speak up in courts and in the face of persecutors, and they received guidance as to where to go to preach the gospel (and where not to go). To take one example, in Acts 13 Paul and Barnabas were commissioned for special missionary work, and the writer notes that the Holy Spirit *told* the Church to commission them and the Holy Spirit *sent* them out.

In the individual lives of faith of these early Christians, the Spirit was indwelling and active, teaching, guiding, sending and actually praying within them. As Paul wrote to the Christians in Rome, 'Likewise the Spirit helps us in our weakness; for we do not know how to pray as we ought, but that very Spirit intercedes with sighs too deep for words' (Rom. 8.26). In Acts and in the letters of Paul and others to the newly emerging churches it is clear that these early Christians experienced the Holy Spirit as power, as truth, as life and as liberty. But supremely the Spirit was experienced as the Spirit of Christ himself, the Spirit of their Lord. The Spirit's presence in each one of them and in their community as a whole was God's self-manifestation in their own lives. The love of God, redeeming and re-creating fallen humanity, once so evident in the earthly life of Jesus, remained present in the world and in the lives of his followers through the Spirit. The promise recorded in John's Gospel (John 14.23), that God would make his home in those who love him, was fulfilled through the in-dwelling presence of the Holy Spirit.

The Holy Spirit and the Church

The Holy Spirit is absolutely central in Christian living and faith. When we talk about the Spirit, we are not discussing an arid or academic doctrine. Rather, in the most intimate way, our understanding of the Spirit is our understanding of the way God makes a home within those who love him. It is also the way that

God acts on and within God's people, continuing the work of creation and re-creation. The sort of words that Christians use to describe this experience are abiding, indwelling, guiding, inspiring and empowering. Above all the Spirit is sheer gift – the gift of the presence of God's very self. It cannot be earned or achieved: it is poured out as grace by God in love. Those who dare to receive this gift, as those early followers in the New Testament, experience it as giving new life and freedom to serve God and God's world, and as enabling them to pray with realism and depth. For it is this Spirit, present within us and our world, that enables us to pray from the depth of our being, even when we don't have the precise words to do so.

It is no wonder that many Christian forms of worship that mark new beginnings in the life of individuals and communities seek the Spirit's presence. Christians sing the ancient hymn *Veni Creator Spiritus* (literally: 'Come, Creator Spirit'), which begins by asking the Spirit to come into the lives of those present: 'Come Holy Ghost, our souls inspire, and lighten with celestial fire.' The Spirit is intimately connected therefore with the sacraments as the experience of Christ at his baptism, the promise of Christ to be present when people gather in his name, and as the lives of the earliest Christians attest. For Jesus, the Spirit descended on him at his baptism. In the early Church, we saw that baptism and the laying on of hands by elders for the gift of the Spirit were closely linked in time. And even when, in later centuries within many branches of the Church, including Roman Catholicism and Anglicanism, the laying on of hands became separated, the Spirit was still present. As infant baptism became the norm, the laying on of hands or 'confirmation' was reserved for a later date when young people could understand their faith more deeply and answer for themselves. In the words of the 1662 Book of Common

Prayer, this service was for those who had reached 'years of discretion'. In most traditions confirmation or a similar rite is the mark of being accepted as a communicant – one who could receive the sacrament of Holy Communion or the Eucharist. Receiving the Holy Spirit at baptism is central to becoming a Christian. It is the entrance into the Church and receiving the very life of Christ, enabling us to live in the way he lived.

But the Spirit is not a private gift, not just the source of individual life in Christ. The presence of God's Spirit creates and binds the Church together as the body of Christ on earth. Without the Holy Spirit, there is no Church – only a human institution, an organization like many others. But with the power and presence of the Holy Spirit the Church becomes the community in which the love and grace of God is poured out through worship, through hearing and preaching Scripture, and through the celebration of the sacraments. Indeed, in a deep and powerful sense the sacraments are the primary way in which this gift is poured out on the specificities of human need. As we see more fully in Chapter 9, Holy Communion (also called the Eucharist or the Mass), when Christians obey Jesus' command to 'do this' in memory of him – to offer, bless, break and eat bread, and to offer, bless and drink wine – provides nourishment for the daily journey of Christian life. Ordination prays for the empowering of the Holy Spirit for new priests and deacons. Marriage similarly invokes the grace of God through the Holy Spirit as a couple enter into a new calling and a new state of life. Reconciliation (also known as confession and absolution) gives reassurance of forgiveness and empowering grace, through the power of the Spirit, to those who are conscious of their sin and their need for constant conversion; and anointing with holy oil seeks the presence and comfort of God's Spirit and brings strength and healing to the sick in mind as well as in body.

The specificity of God's grace outpoured to us in the sacraments emphasizes that the gift of the Holy Spirit cannot be generalized. What we receive through the Spirit is a gift specific to the needs of those who follow Christ, and its 'fruits' are manifested in practical and social ways in the everyday life of the Christian community. Undoubtedly early Christian belief and experience drew on Jewish teaching about the nature of the Spirit of God. Isaiah's prophecy about the coming servant of the Lord spoke of the Spirit of the Lord resting upon him, 'the spirit of wisdom and understanding, the spirit of counsel and might, the spirit of knowledge and the fear of the LORD' (Isa. 11.2). In the New Testament Paul supremely elaborates on the gifts or fruits of the Spirit – how one can tell that those who claim to be Christian are really living lives infused with the love of Christ. Addressing very specific problems within the Galatian church, Paul contrasts a life lived according to 'the desires of the flesh' marked by idolatry, anger, jealousy, envy, dissensions and sexual sin, with lives lived 'by the spirit'. As Paul spells out for us, 'the fruit of the Spirit is love, joy, peace, patience, kindness, generosity, faithfulness, gentleness, and self-control' (Gal. 5.22–23). These 'fruits' are qualities of heart and patterns of interaction with others that reflect God's love. They are also intensely social. There is no idea here that the indwelling of the Holy Spirit is about individual spiritual achievement. Rather, the Spirit gives gifts of heart and mind that build up the Christian family, that express the continued presence of Christ's love in the world.

So the gift of the Holy Spirit is not an invitation to selfish or individual spiritual self-improvement. Of course, it leads to individual change, but it is a gift that overflows into compassion and care for others – love, patience, kindness, goodness, faithfulness, gentleness. Specific gifts of the Spirit are for the common good, for the building up and strengthening of others as part of the body of Christ, which is the Church. We see this clearly once again with Paul where, when writing to the church in Corinth, he speaks of gifts of wisdom, knowledge, faith, healing, and so on. All of these gifts are for the building up of the community of those who are being changed into Christlikeness (1 Cor. 12–14). There were clearly some in Corinth who hankered after dramatic gifts, particularly 'speaking in tongues'. But Paul is resolutely down to earth and practical, and warns the Corinthian Christians against a competitive spirituality that tries to set some believers with certain gifts above others within the church. Using the imagery of the human body, he reminds them that the body needs all its parts with their particular functions to work properly as a whole. Moreover, those parts of the body that seem weaker or less glamorous or less honourable are particularly important to the whole. The body of Christ on earth, the Church, functions in the same organic and mutually dependent way and Paul tells those who believe that 'you are the body of Christ and individually members of it'. What this means practically is that 'God has appointed in the church first apostles, second prophets, third teachers; then deeds of power, then gifts of healing, forms of assistance, forms of leadership, various kinds of tongues' (1 Cor. 12.27–28). The Church needs all of these gifts, given by the Spirit, since not all are prophets and not all are teachers, but all gifts are needed for the building up of the body. Clearly Christians need one another, with the gifts of the Spirit given to each in particular. Paul then goes on to expound the 'more excellent way' – the way of love – in what must be one of the most famous chapters in the New Testament, 1 Corinthians 13. Here Paul states without reserve the centrality of love, even – and especially – for those who have received the Spirit: 'If I speak in the tongues of mortals and of angels, but do not have love, I am a noisy gong or a clanging cymbal' (1 Cor. 13.1). God's Spirit, and the gifts of that Spirit, are made manifest through love so that, of faith, hope and love, Paul can be certain that 'the greatest of these is love' (1 Cor. 13.13).

Life in the Spirit, life empowered, purified and illumined by the Spirit, is pre-eminently life marked by and lived within the love of God. The love of God is 'poured into our hearts through the Holy Spirit' (Rom. 5.5). As we have seen throughout, this Spirit is not just endowment and gift 'from outside'. The Spirit makes its home deep within the hearts and lives of those who love God, transforming, renewing and strengthening them – fashioning the life of Christ in them. This has been the experience of Christians through the centuries, despite individual sin and the failures of the Church. The daily experience of the Spirit in prayer, in community, in Scripture and in the sacraments has been a comfort to Christians across the centuries – and of course still is. This is perhaps stated most clearly in the prayer of a late Medieval mystic that is now a hymn found in many Christian traditions:

Come down, O Love divine,
seek thou this soul of mine,
and visit it with thine own ardour glowing;
O Comforter, draw near, within my heart appear,
and kindle it, thy holy flame bestowing.

O let it freely burn, till earthly passions turn
to dust and ashes in its heat consuming;
And let thy glorious light
shine ever on my sight,
And clothe me round, the while my path illuming.

Let holy charity mine outward vesture be,
and lowliness become mine inner clothing:
True lowliness of heart,
which takes the humbler part,
And o'er its own shortcomings weeps with loathing.

And so the yearning strong,
with which the soul will long,
Shall far outpass the power of human telling;
For none can guess its grace,
till he become the place
Wherein the Holy Spirit makes His dwelling.[1]

Further Reading

Castelo, Daniel (2015), *Pneumatology: A Guide for the Perplexed*, London: Bloomsbury.

Carroll, John T. (2018), *The Holy Spirit in the New Testament*, Nashville, TN: Abingdon Press.

Congar, Yves (2000), *I Believe in the Holy Spirit*, New York: Crossroad.

Ramsey, Michael (1977), *Holy Spirit*, London: SPCK.

Williams, Rowan (2016), *Being Disciples: Essentials of the Christian Life*, London: SPCK. (See especially Chapter 6 on 'Life in the Spirit'.)

.

---

1 Bianco da Siena, 1434, 'Come down, O Love divine' in *The New English Hymnal*, no. 137.

5

Love Personified – The Incarnation

Jarred Mercer

The incarnation: meeting God in Jesus Christ

Christians do not have a preconceived notion of who God is. We do not have a philosophical formula or a definition of who or what God is or is like. What we do have is a God who does not remain far off and distant, a God who comes to us. God *shows up* in Jesus Christ. Therefore, if we want to know what God is like, if we want to know what it means to be divine, we look to Jesus. Christ's life, love, power and grace show us what God's life, love, power and grace are like, because in Christ God has entered into and inhabited human life. God is in Jesus walking among us, touching with human hands. God is in Jesus walking among us and is by human hands touched.

This is in essence what we are saying when we use the word 'incarnation'. The word comes from the Latin *incarnari*, which means 'to be made flesh'. In Christ God is 'enfleshed'. This seems to many impossible, or at least ridiculous. But it is only impossible if God is seen to be really just a big creature: God's power is like our power, just infinitely greater. Or, God's love looks precisely like ours, just stronger, and so on. When two created things try to inhabit the same space, one is displaced, pushed out. Place something in a full glass of water and it overflows; try to shove another apple into a fruit bowl that is already filled to the brim with them, and another apple will come toppling out. But even though much of theology these days, and most preaching, speaks of God or God's actions in the world in a way – without intending to do so – that sounds as if God is a giant person with characteristics like ours only perfected, this is not in any way the Christian view of God. In fact, it is actually not the view of God in any theistic religion.

God is no creature. God is not a *thing*, not part of the created order, and is therefore not in competition with it. Things aren't displaced when God is present with them (and God is always present with them). Water isn't overflowing, apples aren't toppling. And so God is free to move and act in the world at all times without friction. This is simply a description of God working in creation generally, one we have seen discussed already in Chapter 3. The particularity of the incarnation is different, but the principle of God not being in competition with creation, not vying for position or space, remains. So, when God unites divinity with humanity in a particular human person, Jesus Christ, it might indeed at first sight seem weird or ridiculous, but if God is God, there is nothing that is beyond reason or possibility here. It would indeed be *un*reasonable for God not to be free to do so, as if God were a created thing competing for space with other created things. Humans cannot rival God, we are not on a level playing field with divinity, and so divinity can perfectly coexist with humanity in Christ without one overtaking the other. If created things are created things and God is God, full humanity and full divinity can happily dwell together in Christ without one decreasing so that the other might increase.

This is what we're saying is happening in the person of Christ. The fullness of God and the fullness of humanity are united in one person. But why? We will get to the true significance of why in a moment, but why would people even begin to say this? Why have Christians insisted that Jesus Christ is divine?

Jesus is human in every way that we are. He learned from his parents, was fed at his mother's breast, got tired and annoyed just like we do. But he is also the place in the world, the presence in the world, where people recognize God. Jesus is 'Emmanuel', God with us. And people recognize God in Jesus Christ throughout his life, from before his birth to his resurrection, even if no one fully understood what this meant until his time on earth was finished. Here is the human life, the whole human life, that reveals God to us. From the time of Christ's appearing people have watched his living, his dying, and his rising and have recognized God in their midst. Jesus lives a human life that is at every step also divine life.

The emphasis on the whole life of Christ is really important. People (including theologians and preachers) often talk about the incarnation as just a cute Christmas story, a necessary step in the journey towards the really important parts of Christ's life (typically the cross and resurrection). But talk about God enfleshed in Jesus, about Emmanuel, is not talk about a singular instance in Christ's life. God was not enfleshed only as the baby Jesus in a manger surrounded by adorable farm animals. To speak of the incarnation is to speak about the entire human existence of Christ – from birth, to his perfect obedient life, to his death, resurrection, ascension, and coming again. Through his entire existence, through all of it, this is where we meet God-with-us.

True God and true human: love personified

In the incarnation, when God enters our humanity in Christ, God is sharing with us God's eternal self-knowledge and understanding. This is what we mean by revelation. How God eternally knows and loves within God's own self as Father, Son and Holy Spirit is communicated, shared with us, in a way that we can actually understand. We can know something of the unknowable and infinite, the one who is always infinitely beyond our understanding, not because God can be figured out, not because we can conjure up the right answer about who God is, but simply because this unsearchable infinite one has shown up. Because of God's appearing.

The incarnation is absolutely necessary for us to truly know and love God because God cannot be known in the abstract. Actually, we cannot know anything in the abstract! All of our knowledge is knowledge in context, knowledge that is grounded in the reality of our lives. Even if it is knowledge of timeless things, it is known by us, it is understood within our bodies and minds, and in relation to other things that we know or experience. So we cannot actually know anything in a non-historical, other-worldly, vacuum; but this is particularly true in the case of knowing God, who is not a part of the created universe, who is not body and mind and in relation to other things like us. God can never be a theory. And so God comes to us in Christ so that we can know God in the only way that we can know anything at all, as humans.

This is why Jesus is called the Word of God in Scripture. Jesus is the 'Word', because he communicates God's 'God-ness' to us, indeed, he communicates God to us. Jesus is God translated into human life and understanding. He is God's very life entering human history. And when that life shows up with and among us it is nothing other than a manifestation of love. The life of Jesus Christ, from the humility of the manger to the agony of the cross to the glory of heaven, is a life of self-gift, a life of true and unending love. We know that 'God is love' (1 John 4.8) because it is Jesus who shows us most fully who God is, and Jesus is all and only love. Jesus Christ is perfect divine love present in our world. He is love personified.

There is nowhere that we see clearer the senselessness of God's love than in the life of Christ. Love in Christ means the Messiah is born in a stable, sinners are welcome at the table, lepers are embraced, the king is crowned on a cross, and life comes from death. Jesus reveals God to us, and in Jesus we see the divine life and love rejected, made a refugee, homeless, criminalized, power-less, defeated, dead. The whole world comes undone, and God re-creates a world born again out of perfect, self-giving love.

What makes our God of incarnation even more beautiful is that we not only find God here, but we also find ourselves. Christ as fully God, and also fully human in every way that we are, is the fulfilment of our humanity. We were created for union with God; we exist for Love. And in Christ, all that it means to be God is united to all that it means to be human, and so the human condition is finally and fully welcomed into its perfection – makes its way home to union with God.

Jesus, who lives in perfect obedience to God – who loves perfectly – is the human person as all human persons were meant to be. He is the true human. He is not only fully human in every way that we are, but the perfect human as all of us should be. And so in the incarnation, Jesus unites the divine life to our everyday, mundane humanity and brings us to where we have always intended to be: happiness, heaven, whatever name we put to it.

The incarnation is a welcome into God's perfect love, and it is to be truly human.

The great twentieth-century theologian Karl Barth wrote, 'We do not need to engage in a free-ranging investigation to seek out and construct who and what God truly is, and who and what man truly is, but only to read the truth about both where it resides, namely, in the fullness of their togetherness, their covenant which proclaims itself in Jesus Christ' (Barth, 1960, p. 47). The incarnate Christ is God and humanity's togetherness, and as such is our salvation and fullness.

The new humanity: learning to live in love

So what does this really mean for our lives now? It is thrilling to be loved, and to know that one is headed for the fullness of that love, but we've already established that God's love does not come to us in the abstract; it touches down in the reality of our lives. So how is this new human existence in Christ present with and in us now?

To meet Christ, to be counted as Christ's, is to enter this new life of love. It doesn't mean that we're perfect (surely!), it doesn't even mean that we are very good at living in that new life yet, but Christ's continued presence with us through the Holy Spirit in the life of the Church is an invitation into it nonetheless. Dietrich Bonhoeffer said that Christ stands 'beyond my existence, but still for me' (Bonhoeffer, p. 61; quoted in Williams, 2000, p. 91). The process of Christian life is a process of growing beyond who we are now and into our true selves in Christ. Jesus renews our entire vision of what it means to be a human being, and in doing so changes the direction of our lives. He does not only show us what true humanity is, but he is also the way to that fullness. He is the paradigm for us to follow.

But as he himself truly inhabits our human condition, he has also already performed the journey, already brought what it is to be a human into the divine love. So the way is already accomplished; our true self (Jesus) has accomplished the task, and in doing so has become the path for each of us to follow. Christ is himself our new life, but also makes new life possible for each of us. From the manger to the cross, he has entered into the depths of our brokenness and despair, our shame and insecurity, and he welcomes all of it. He unites all of it to God's perfect life and love. And because Christ did this from within human life, the possibilities for human life have been expanded: we are no longer slaves to sin, but alive in freedom and righteousness (Rom. 6.18).

God's ways are not our ways (Isa. 55.8–9), and Jesus has united our ways to God's so that our self-serving and inward-focused lives are opened up to new possibilities. A new way of human life has come to us, been shown to us, and we are invited into it. *Divine* generosity and love has been embodied and lived out in *human* life. And this changes everything.

Our lives are more complicated than we think. We are not simply individuals; we are not free to be who we are or want to be or make all our own decisions, no matter how loudly the popular imagination contends that this is the case. We are shaped by our surroundings in nearly every conceivable way. From infancy we are being moulded through our families, friends, language, culture, religion, and the decisions of others into our world's brokenness.

This enculturation into brokenness makes a life lived in love with and towards God in Christ, a life of accepting rather than rejecting God's love, nearly if not definitively impossible. We are from the very beginning formed by what has been called a 'climate of disobedience' to God (Williams, 2015, p. 5). This is a description of what Christians have often called original sin, which is not necessarily an inheritance of guilt for sin (though many Christians have interpreted it this way), but rather a living network of the rejection of God's purposes in the world, of God's love in the world, present long before we come along. And when we do come along it is a network we enter into before we've even had the chance to do anything at all, much less sin.

We are stuck in a history, a family story, of rejecting God's free gift of love, and it is this rejection of love we call sin. We were made by and for love, and desire love, but we perpetually reject it; and in the end when perfect Love stands before us in our midst, we even crucify it. We are enslaved in our disobedience, our visceral and violent response to God's gifts. When Jesus comes, when God enters this murky human history, he inaugurates a new sort of human life, he offers a new response to God's love – he offers humanity a posture of acceptance rather than rejection of God's love. In living a life of perfect obedience to and in love, Jesus carves out a new path for us by living out God's love perfectly rather than rejecting it, as all other humans have done in some way.

This is precisely how our state of sinfulness is reversed. How, in the words of the Letter to the Ephesians, the old self is taken off and the new self is put on (Eph. 4.22–24). Christ enters our very humanity, unites us to himself, carries us through his perfect life, takes our broken human condition to the cross, and brings it through death into resurrected, transfigured, transformed, new life. So that in Christ, everything we thought we knew about ourselves, our world, and God is entirely subverted, even crucified. 'You have died', Scripture says, 'and your life is hidden with Christ in God' (Col. 3.3).

Participation in this full incarnate life of Christ is our salvation. Salvation is not just forgiveness of sins, a second chance, or living for ever in an afterlife. Salvation is union with God in Christ. Christ unites our humanity to divinity and carries it through life, death and resurrection into union with God in the life of the Trinity. This is what I mean by the incarnation not just being a cute Christmas story. The incarnation is our *whole* story.

The incarnation is not only a movement of descent: God to us. It is also an ascent: us to God. God coming to us to dwell among us in our brokenness would make for a compassionate and empathetic God, but not a God who saves. The God of our salvation doesn't just come to us in Christ, identify with our suffering, and then leave us there in it. He brings us out. Christ carries our humanity to new life in the eternal love of God. This is why Christians have always spoken of the incarnation as not only God entering our humanity but humanity entering into divinity: 'God became human that humanity might become divine' has always been the dictum of our salvation, though some corners of modern Christianity seem to have forgotten this. Indeed, this reality that is so central to our faith, to many Christian ears today sounds scandalous. But we're not saying that people become 'gods'. It is simply to agree with Scripture in 2 Peter 1.4, which says that through Christ we 'become partakers of the divine nature'. As Christ enters into our humanity in the incarnation (partaking in human nature), so we are welcomed and embraced into God's eternal love as Father, Son and Holy Spirit (partaking of the divine nature). In the person of Jesus Christ, humanity and divinity are literally united for all eternity, and in Christ – as those who belong to Christ – we share in that unity.

God in infancy: the vulnerability of love

While a theology of the incarnation is not just concerned with the initial point that Christ is enfleshed in our human history, the story of Christmas has a lot to tell us about what it means for God to be incarnate. The promised Messiah, for whom God's people had been waiting for centuries, comes to redeem the world. Reasonably, the magi, or 'wise men' as they are often called, search for him in the palace. He isn't there, of course, but this is what makes the most sense. When a king is born, you don't search for him among haystacks and animal waste. But that is where we find him, outside the city, outside even a house or inn. The promised Messiah, who was coming to redeem the world, enters this life not from the high pedigree of the aristocracy and not into a family of other kings as one among many in a line of rulers, but through the womb of a lowly and disgraced unwed peasant girl. The Messiah, the world's redeemer, comes not with public fanfare and parades and parties, shouting and dancing and celebration, but in the stillness and cover of night, visited by poor shepherds. Christ is born and delegates do not visit to negotiate trade agreements or arrange a marriage in an effort to keep order and peace. The world order is indeed so threatened by this infant that the powers that be order the execution of any child that might even resemble him and he must flee a terrorist regime and become a refugee in a foreign land. (If our current political situation teaches us anything, it is that there is nothing more threatening to the powerful in our world than the poor, vulnerable and marginalized.)

Poor, rejected, excluded, tiny, weak, defenceless, cast out as a national security risk – here is where we find God's love among us. Here is love personified. God in Christ has entered humanity at its smallest, earliest, weakest, most vulnerable state, and this is the hope of our salvation. For here it becomes immediately clear, from the very beginning of Christ's life as he inhabits our weakness and poverty, that there is no reality, no experience or place in which we can be, where God's love is not found. God's love is present with us in utter dependence and frailty, even the fragility of infancy. And further, in the fear of a young mother, in our 'otherness' and rejection, in every darkness that infects humanity, oppresses or takes advantage of those who are weak, in every cry for help, the perfect, unending, love of God is present: *Emmanuel*, God is with us.

The manner of Christ's incarnation, the humility and lowliness of it all, shows us that God's love is a love without borders. There is no place it refuses to go. And this means that all of our frailty and brokenness has been met with God's love in Christ. As the Letter to the Hebrews has it, he has shared in our very flesh and blood, become our kin, like us in every respect, so that he might become our 'merciful and faithful high priest', and we might be freed from slavery (Heb. 2.17).

God's borderless love in the incarnation means not only that there is no situation in our life beyond the reach of God's love, but also that no person is beyond that love. Christ as our kin in the incarnation means Christ is kin to the most vile as much as the most lovely. The knowledge that we are loved by this boundless love grants to us great freedom, but also calls us to live a life of borderless love as Christ does. Every person is to be seen by those sharing in Christ's new humanity as someone to whom Jesus Christ is kin and God is Father (Barth, 1960, p. 53). And if they live in such a way as to communicate that they do not yet understand who they are, then it is our job to make it clear to them, to show them how marvellous a love has met them in Christ.

God's love present in the manger reveals God's love to be everywhere. This is a love with no borders and without hesitations. A love personified, made real in our humanity, in our weakest and most vulnerable state. Emmanuel – God with us in infancy, in poverty, in loneliness, in fear. God with us in the face of the suffering. God with us, the light shining in our darkness that darkness cannot overcome.

Further Reading

Athanasius of Alexandria, trans. and intro. by John Behr, 2001, *On the Incarnation*, New York: St Vladimir's Seminary Press.

Behr, John (2013), *Becoming Human: Meditations on Christian Anthropology in Word and Image*, New York: St Vladimir's Seminary Press.

Bonhoeffer, Dietrich (1966), *Christology*, trans. John Bowden, London: Collins.

Macquarrie, John (2003), *Stubborn Theological Questions*, London: SCM Press.

Spence, Alan (2008), *Christology: A Guide for the Perplexed,* London: Bloomsbury.

Tanner, Kathryn (2001), *Jesus, Humanity and the Trinity,* Minneapolis, MN: Fortress Press.

Williams, Rowan (2014), *Meeting God in Mark*, London: SPCK.

6

Love Negated – Sin and Suffering

Jonathan Jong and Peter Groves

God is love, and loves us. On this hangs all of Christian theology (and, as you may have noticed, the preceding chapters of this book), just as all of the law hangs on the commandments to love God and neighbour. Even the Christian doctrines of sin, evil and suffering are essentially meditations on the love of God. Specifically, sin is, in the final analysis, the negation of the love of God: it is the rejection of the love that brings us into being and gives us life, the love who is born to us in Jesus, and that inspires us to love by the power of the Holy Spirit. All of which is to say that we cannot really talk about sin without first talking about *goodness*.

What is good?

A good toaster is one that consistently toasts bread to the desired level of crispness. A good apple tree is one that grows and blossoms and produces fruit in due season. A good doctor is one who more often than not makes accurate diagnoses and provides effective treatments, all the while being a comforting presence to the patient and their loved ones. Goodness comes in many forms. People disagree about what exactly it is that makes something good: this should not come as a surprise to anyone. Some people think that what makes something good is when it increases the amount of happiness in the world. Assuming that it makes sense to talk about *amounts* of happiness, we can see that our good toaster, apple tree and doctor are plausible candidates for things that increase happiness – for example, for toast-eating breakfasters, apple-eating squirrels, and children with flu. Others disagree, pointing out that this reliance on happiness can only apply when there are sentient beings around who can be said to enjoy things: but it would seem that a healthy growing and fruitful tree is a good tree even in an animal-free wood. In any case, this view has not proved very popular among Christians thinkers who have, throughout the Church's history, written about such things. However, it is currently a very influential idea. Modern societies seem obsessed with happiness. We have even made great efforts to quantify and measure happiness, as a means of evaluating how well different countries are doing: perhaps this is preferable to our previous preoccupation with economic productivity as enshrined in measures of gross domestic product.

Christians have generally maintained that what makes something good has a lot to do with the something itself, specifically its nature. The nature of a thing is whatever it is that makes it that thing, without which it would no longer be that thing. For example, something that looks like a toaster but does not make toast is not really a toaster at all: it may once have been a toaster, but it is now junk, or a toaster-shaped ornament. Furthermore, if it does make toast, but poorly, it is a bad toaster. We must be careful not to extrapolate too much from this example – to think that the nature of a thing is always its *function*. For one thing, not everything has a function in the way that toasters have functions: toasters were invented and are manufactured to make toast. Apple trees, to bring back another example, do not exist to provide food for squirrels. They exist for their own good: or, as Kant might say, they are not means to some other end, but ends in themselves. In other words, their purpose is to flourish, which – for an apple tree – probably involves growth and reproduction in an ecosystem in equilibrium.

Sin: choosing other than what is good

As we have already seen in Chapter 3, human beings also exist not for the benefit or pleasure of any other creature, but for our own sakes. Recall that our value and integrity are grounded in the love of God, who created us and whose perfection means that God cannot gain anything from us or, indeed, from any other created thing. This is the theological foundation of the world's – and therefore, humanity's – intrinsic worth. Like the apple tree, then, our purpose is to flourish. Unlike the apple tree, however, we exercise a degree of agency upon our flourishing. Apple trees do not, except in a metaphorical way, choose to receive sunlight and water, even though their branches might grow towards the sun and their roots might grow to reach moisture in the earth. If the apple tree is bad – if it wilts or fails to produce fruit – it is not because it has chosen to do so. In contrast, we make choices all the time that contribute to our flourishing, or – to bring us closer to the topic of this chapter – impede it: we can choose to eat crisps rather than carrots, to breathe city smog rather than the fresh air of the countryside, to binge watch the latest box set rather than go for a brisk walk. Our choices go beyond the physiological, of course: we can also choose to be cruel rather than kind, to read tabloid magazines rather than the Bible, to go to the casino rather than the bank, thus compromising our moral, spiritual, and economic flourishing.

This is what sin is, then: choosing other than what is good for us. Sin does not always involve choosing to act wickedly: sometimes, it is a matter of choosing the lesser good. There does not have to be anything inherently evil about crisps or cities or celebrity 'news' or casinos for it to be sinful to choose them over things that are actually good for us, that contribute to our flourishing, the fulfilment of our natures. Furthermore, what counts as the greater and lesser good often depends on the situation: it is not always better to go for a brisk walk than to relax in front of the television. Occasionally, of course, sin does involve choosing to act wickedly: even then, it is a choice to act wickedly rather than justly, which is the better of the two both for the victims of our actions but also, crucially, for ourselves. Our cruelty affects other people, and compromises their flourishing, but it also violates our own nature and thwarts the good purposes God has for us. Our purpose, you will not be surprised to hear, is to love: or, it is to enjoy God who glories in us, which amounts to the same thing. The summary of the Law and the summary of Christian faith meet, after all.

Sin: a case of mistaken identity

It is not obvious that our purpose is to love, especially given what Christians say love looks like. As we learned in Chapter 2, the love of God looks like the Father, Son, and Spirit pouring themselves out into one another without remain, leaving nothing back of themselves to one another. Also as Chapter 5 reminded us, the love of God looks like the creator of the universe being born in a manger, suffering alongside the oppressed and marginalized, offering a balm for wracked bodies and woeful souls. It looks like death on a cross, and yet forgiving those who tortured and murdered him. Love is costly: it demands everything of us. Nothing in our evolutionary heritage and cultural inheritance makes it easy to love. In a world where self-preservation and self-propagation are incentivized, love is more often than not the counterintuitive choice. No wonder then that we, more often than not, choose other than to love; instead, we choose lesser goods like safety and security, comfort and convenience. The love that God offers is without condition, it precedes everything, is the very foundation of our existence, and is unaffected by even the most shameful facts of our lives. But the life that God's love offers is hard in this world as we have made it; according to how our desires have been formed, it is simply unattractive.

Sin is therefore first a kind of ignorance, a blindness to the good. The imagery of light and darkness in John's Gospel and the other Johannine writings make this point (e.g. John 1.1–5; 3.19–20; 1 John 1.5–7). Sometimes this ignorance is honest: we really just do not know how to want the right things, like children who prefer eating sweets over vegetables or the voter who supports the bigot because they think he will take their family out of financial insecurity. Sometimes this ignorance is wilful, as when we just do not want to know about the working conditions under which our clothes are made, or food grown. But more fundamentally than a failure of recognition of the good external to ourselves, sin is a blindness to a truth about ourselves: that we are very good, as the book of Genesis 1.31 declares it. As most good psychotherapists will observe, our desperate desire for self-preservation and self-enhancement – even at the expense of others

– is a symptom of deep insecurity, the fear that our worth and value is predicated on something beyond the sheer miracle of our existence. We believe that we are – without the trappings of life as it is sold to us through commercials or box sets or our covetous imaginations of how much happier our neighbours are than ouselves– *nothing*. This is a kind of atheism: the belief that if we are not 'self-made' people then we are nothing is the rejection of our createdness, a denial that God has done the work of loving us into being.

To say that sin is in the first place a kind of ignorance – even a kind of atheism – may seem to give too much weight to the sorts of intellectual things that academic theologians and philosophers obsess about; a far cry from the messy embodied and emotional reality of sin as we experience it in daily life. But the kind of ignorance that sin is turns out not just to be an in-accuracy about some obscure historical matter or some abstruse semantic distinction. Rather, it is the failure to realize that we are loved, which produces the fear that we are unloved or, worse still, unlovable. As much as Christian living involves self-sacrifice – our paradigm of love, as we find it in John 15.13 ('No one has greater love than this, to lay down one's life for one's friends') and witness it in the death of Jesus – it actually begins with self-love, which is the proper product of the love of God for us and the source of our love for others, as in the second of the great com-mandments, to love our neighbours *as ourselves* (Matt. 22.35–40; Mark 12.28–34). In so far as this failure to love ourselves leads us to choose things that diminish and damage us, as it often and perhaps inevitably does, then sin is a form of self-harm.

Sin: the metastasizing of self-harm

We fail to recognize ourselves as God sees us, and consequently fail to love ourselves properly, which is to say, without condition. Rather, we condition our love for ourselves on our attributes and achievements, usually on the basis of what our culture tells us to value and desire. Cultural standards of beauty and productivity become our canons of what it is to be a successful human being. Power and wealth, security and convenience become the objects of our desire. There is, of course, nothing wrong with wanting to feel safe or financially secure. But our reliance on these things for our sense of meaning and self-esteem too easily and too often descend into fetishization and idolatry, and they prove to be gods as fickle as the markets in which they now operate. Hence, the anxious covetousness of keeping up with the Joneses, the insecurely attached parenthood of those who seek to live vicariously through their offspring, the exploitation of labour and the natural environment for the sake of our material comfort, and other such maladies that may seem modern, but have always plagued us in one guise or another.

Judgemental busybodies who pontificate about the sinfulness of self-harm and suicide have things the wrong way around. We moralize and medicalize these behaviours, but this belies the fact that they are really just acute and poignant examples of the human proclivity for self-inflicted suffering so widespread as to be banal. Consider our habits, in our personal lives no less than in global geopolitics, of escalating conflict over expressing compassion for fear of seeming weak. In our perverted pride, we prefer arms races and strategies of mutually assured destruction over true peace. Or consider the sacrifices we make on the altar of our careers – sleep and exercise, time with our loved ones – for the sake of more and more of newer, shinier things that we have convinced ourselves are the necessities of modern life, but that we did not even know we wanted until we saw advertisements for them. Or, worse still, meaningless job titles and the envy of co-workers and competitors, which we mistake for esteem.

Already, we can see how sin spreads suffering, how our failure to realize our value, bestowed upon us without condition by God who gives us being, makes us miserable with insecurity that then compels us to enhance ourselves in ways that adversely affect others. There is another way to think about this that makes the scale of sin and suffering more obvious. Our failure to recognize the truth about ourselves is a tragic case of mistaken identity. Rather than finding ourselves in the love of God, we seek to find versions of ourselves to love in other, lesser terms. We construct identities as workers and consumers, as members of families and ethnic groups and nation-states and religious organizations. There is nothing wrong with taking pride in our work or enjoying the fruits of others' ingenuity and labour; nor with celebrating one's ethnic origin or national character; nor, of course, with being particularly devout. But all these things are easily perverted, even accidentally by disordered prioritization, into workaholism and wasteful consumerism, and varieties of fundamentalist extremism, whether ethno-nationalist or religious.

Furthermore, having considered ourselves primarily as workers or lovers or whatever, we inevitably also see and value others by this light. This has two effects. The first is that we objectify and instrumentalize them: we treat them like cogs in machines, if not of our own making then of the making of the company or the state or the Church. We fail to see – or care – that the voice on the other end of the helpline is a person, loved by God, which is to say absolutely lovable; as is the celebrity, whose private life we consume with envy or mockery; as is the spouse whose sacrifices we have taken for granted for years, promising ourselves that we'll make it up to them one day, perhaps after we retire from our high-flying careers that have left beds cold and birthdays missed. The second is that we resent the ways in which they differ from us, for fear that different means better, and therefore that we might be worse: worse at our jobs or marriages, or at the lottery of our circumstances, our skin colour, our nationality, our sexual orientation. As social scientists and any astute observer of human behaviour can testify, the most prevalent way of dealing with this is to assert our superiority whenever we detect difference, not least by denigrating those different from us to predictable effect. Sin is the banal thing of failing to know that we are loved, but its impact on the world is demonstrably catastrophic.

It is tempting to distinguish between the mundane sins we commit – lying to our parents, being rude to the waiter, neglecting our spouse – and the evil perpetrated by despots, psychopaths, and estate agents. And of course we are not all Hitler or Charles Manson, Pol Pot or Harold Shipman. But then again, not all atrocities are committed by clinically diagnosable individuals. In contrast, it is not at all obvious that we – ordinary people, who think of ourselves as decent – are immune from the corrupting effects of power. Furthermore, even if it is true that we could never be architects of large-scale violence we undeniably participate in and perpetuate systems that inflict suffering upon thousands upon thousands of people whom we are unlikely to ever meet. We do so, not because we are ignorant – most of us have heard of sweatshops and blood diamonds – but because the system benefits us: it guarantees the lifestyles to which we have grown accustomed, in which food and consumer products are cheap (which also encourages wastage) and we live in peace bought at

the price of blood spilt far from our national borders. We continue
to vote for governments that keep increasing military budgets to
fund ever more efficient methods of killing. We continue to buy
goods – tea, T-shirts, high-tech gadgets – whose supply chains
are tainted by slavery not dissimilar from the phenomenon
William Wilberforce and Abraham Lincoln campaigned against.
Over 200 years later, and there are an estimated 40 million slaves
around the world, according to the International Labour
Organization and the Walk Free Foundation.[2] Chances are, this
information will not radically change your political and consumer
behaviour, nor mine. When it comes down to it, people suffer
and die because of the choices we make daily, because daily we
choose the lesser goods of own comforts and conveniences over
the welfare of others – over love.

We perpetuate these systems and cycles of injustice and violence,
but we did not invent them; we were born and socialized into this
world. It is not only us who are born into such a world, of course;
it is a peculiar form of narcissism to believe that ours is the worst
of times, no less than it is to believe that ours is the best of times.
There is much to protest about the modern nation-state with its
monopoly of violence and the market economy that feeds its
coffers, but if it is not this world that we take for granted, it would
have been another one like it, perhaps with feudal lords rather
than CEOs, boiling oil rather than sarin gas or novichok. All of
which is just to say that our bad choices – and the suffering they
engender in ourselves and others – do not happen in a vacuum,
and do not arise out of us, out of nothing. We are the authors of
our actions, but our compositions are constrained and conditioned

---

2 International Labour Organization and Walk Free Foundation, 2017, *Global
Estimates of Modern Slavery: Forced Labour and Forced Marriage*, Geneva:
ILO Publications. Retrieved from www.ilo.org/wcmsp5/groups/public/@
dgreports/@dcomm/documents/publication/wcms_575479.pdf.

by the world as we have inherited it. In turn, we participate in its construction, and pass it down to our children. This sense that our sins are symptoms of something more fundamentally amiss with the world is what some people call the human condition, and what Christians call original sin.

So far, this chapter has not even mentioned the infamous problem of evil, let alone made an attempt at that enterprise called *theodicy*, the work of – as Milton put it – justifying the ways of God to man. There is a real question here, which leads to a real problem. Why *is* the world such as it is, populated by creatures that suffer so and, perhaps worse still, that inflict so much suffering on themselves and others? Why did God make it so, and why doesn't God do something about it? Throughout the centuries, Christians have provided many answers to these questions, but none of them are quite satisfactory. In fact, some Christian responses are quite reprehensible. Consider, for example, the idea that pain and suffering are often or always instances of divine punishment for human misbehaviour. In recent times, some Christian ministers have claimed in the media that natural disasters, terrorist attacks, and stock market plunges occur because God is angry about homosexuality, or some other thing that they deem sinful. It is hard to know what to make of such a claim, but we might begin by observing that it is a God with poor communication skills who uses a financial crisis to protest against marriage equality.

Another common response is that God permits suffering in order to accomplish some greater good: for example, the suffering of others gives us the opportunity to exercise kindness. This too is morally problematic, not just because the distribution of human suffering is obviously unequal but also because the instrumentalizing of suffering trivializes it by turning it into a premise in a cost-benefit analysis. When John's Gospel has Caiaphas the high priest advise the enraged Pharisees in their plot to kill Jesus by saying 'it is better for you to have one man die for the people than to have the whole nation destroyed' (John 11.50), it is not endorsing the economic rationality of this view. Nor should we think more generally of suffering and death in those terms. There is, however, a related response that goes some way to showing that it is at least *possible* to believe in God given the observation that there is rather a lot of suffering in the world. This is the idea that while God has indeed made a world in which suffering occurs, God did not create the suffering itself. Indeed, no one created the suffering: suffering – or sin, or evil – is not a thing but rather an absence or negation of something, of something good. What God does make is good things, whose interaction might sometimes lead to suffering. Consider, for example, human beings and viruses. It is good for the human being that it exists; and it is good for the virus that it exists; but put them together, and you might get a human being who suffers from flu.

This response leaves many questions unanswered, and may raise more than it answers. We might wonder, for example, whether God could have made human beings and viruses slightly differently, or ensured that they never met. We might wonder more generally whether God could have made a world full of good things that never interacted in ways so as to damage one another. What we do not have, then, is a watertight explanation of God's creative work – that is still beyond our ken. We do, however, know that we are not the only ones to find the world wanting. We are not the only ones who lament our tendency to sin, the pervasiveness of suffering, the finality of death. We know this because of what Jesus accomplishes in his incarnation, ministry, death and re-surrection.

Just as Christians cannot begin to talk about sin without first talking about goodness, nor can we finish talking about sin without insisting that God's love for us cannot so easily be thwarted by our ignorance and belligerence. The God who loves us into being also saves us, even from ourselves. God joins us in our human condition, and goes to hell for us, and back again, to bring us into the good life where we belong. But that is a story for another chapter.

Further Reading

Alison, James (1998), *The Joy of Being Wrong: Original Sin through Easter Eyes*, New York: Crossroad.

Chittister, Joan (2015), *Between the Dark and the Daylight: Embracing the Contradictions of Life*, New York: Image Books.

McCabe, Herbert (2005), 'Original Sin' in B. Davies (ed.), *God Still Matters*, London: Bloomsbury, pp. 166–81.

Williams, Harry A. (1965), 'Conceived and Born in Sin', in *True Wilderness*, London: Continuum.

Williams, Rowan (2010), 'Sinners', in J. Chittister and R. Williams, *Uncommon Gratitude: Alleluia for All That Is*, Collegeville, MD: Liturgical Press, pp. 52–64.

7

Love Enacted – Redemption and the Cross

Peter Groves

In Jesus of Nazareth, we encounter the love of God. As we have been discovering, that love is not something that will fit into our patterns or preconceptions. It is all-embracing and all-encompassing; it is offered without condition or demand. And this fact is something that unsettles us because we know, both from our own experiences and from the world around us, that love and human beings don't always go well together. The history of Christian theology is littered with attempts to explain this awkward truth, attempts which need not concern us very much here. But we do need to acknowledge that being human relates to love in two very important ways: to be human is to be capable of love, and to be human is also to be not as good at loving as we might be.

That simple statement is not intended to be glib. We know all too well that human failures to love have consequences of un-imaginable horror. We have confronted this uncomfortable reality in the previous chapter. Human beings are capable of love, and they are also capable of acts of cruelty and destruction far beyond the experience or imagination of most of us – who are fortunate enough to live in places of relative safety and plenty. But those terrible aspects of being human are not as far removed from the ordinary aspects of being human as we would like. Failure at loving is something characteristic, to some extent at least, of every human person. And so if God is love itself, the failure to love must distance humanity from God.

Can this distance be overcome? The Christian answer is an unequivocal yes, but not for any theoretical or imagined reason. God and humanity can be reconciled because in Jesus Christ they already are. The love of God has transformed, and will transform, human beings because in Jesus the self of humanity is swallowed up in the love that makes no sense. Theologians often talk of this reconciliation in terms of forgiveness. When we encounter the love of God in Jesus, we tend to experience that love in many different human ways. Among the most important of these is as forgiveness because encountering perfect love confronts us immediately with our own imperfections. We are sure we do not belong in a relationship of unconditional love; we are sure there must be a barrier between God and our true selves; and so we construe that barrier as an obstacle for God, a kind of test for God to overcome.

This way of thinking is not as daft as it sounds. After all, forgiveness, as a concept, is not always very popular. Throughout human history, we find that its opposite – revenge – is something glamorous. Of the stories and poems you have heard and read, plays and films that you have seen, consider how many of them are concerned with the desire for vengeance. Many of art's greatest masterpieces – *The Oresteia*, *Hamlet*, *Götterdämmerung* to name but three – revolve around revenge. There are few human urges so basic, and few so self-assuring. Revenge feeds upon the obsessive certainty of one person that they have been wronged, are in the right, and are entitled – by justice – to inflict suffering upon others.

Revenge – glamorous and grimly comforting – is the opposite of forgiveness. And so forgiveness is appropriately unfashionable. In fact, it is something positively fearful. Few things appear to disconcert human beings quite so much as the challenge to forgive. Look at a parable of Jesus:

For this reason the kingdom of heaven may be compared to a king who wished to settle accounts with his slaves. When he began the reckoning, one who owed him ten thousand talents was brought to him; and, as he could not pay, his lord ordered him to be sold, together with his wife and children and all his possessions, and payment to be made. So the slave fell on his knees before him, saying, 'Have patience with me, and I will pay you everything.' And out of pity for him, the lord of that slave released him and forgave him the debt. But that same slave, as he went out, came upon one of his fellow-slaves who owed him a hundred denarii; and seizing him by the throat, he said, 'Pay what you owe.' Then his fellow-slave fell down and pleaded with him, 'Have patience with me, and I will pay you.' But he refused; then he went and threw him into prison until he should pay the debt. When his fellow-slaves saw what had happened, they were greatly distressed, and they went and reported to their lord all that had taken place. Then his lord summoned him and said to him, 'You wicked slave! I forgave you all that debt because you pleaded with me. Should you not have had mercy on your fellow-slave, as I had mercy on you?' And in anger his lord handed him over to be tortured until he should pay his entire debt. (Matt. 18.23–34).

The point is a simple one – the one who does not forgive others has no right to expect forgiveness himself or herself. The relationships that exist in the parable, between the just master and his servant, and between that wicked servant and his own debtor, challenge us to take forgiveness seriously. Human beings are often reluctant to do so, and our reluctance is hardly surprising, when we consider that forgiveness and revenge are ultimately about power, the lack of which is the source of many of our fears. If someone has wronged me, then I have something 'on' that person, as the modern jargon says. I can comfort myself with the knowledge that I stand in a superior moral and even, I might think, spiritual relationship to that person, because they have wronged me in a manner that has not been redressed. They owe me something – a moral debt. And the world owes them something – a just revenge.

If, on the other hand, I manage in this case to live out the teaching of Jesus that I find in the Gospel, and offer genuine forgiveness to the person who has wronged me, I have lost that position of power and superiority. I am owed nothing. I have given something that I didn't need to give – forgiveness – and I have gained nothing in return. This is not the way that our petty desires for personal power and for self-assurance tell us that we ought to behave. To forgive someone is to take a risk, the risk of returning to a relationship of equals, of rejoining that person on a level moral playing field, and taking the chance that the wrong will be repeated or, worse, that I will do wrong myself, without now bearing any smug self-satisfaction that, because the person is in my debt, I am entitled to do them harm.

To renounce any relationship of power is unsettling for us human beings, counterintuitive to all that tends to govern the way we act. For anyone truly to forgive is, strangely, even more unsettling than the simple giving up of a power play. The problem for us is that if we freely remit the wrongs committed against us by others, we have acknowledged, by our own actions, that forgiveness is something possible. Not only something possible, but something freely given that the recipient has little power to do anything about. If we live out the freedom of forgiveness with the irrational love that Jesus exhorts, we are doing something very frightening indeed. We are acknowledging that others might freely forgive us, however false and inadequate we know we are ourselves. More to the point, we are acknowledging that it is possible for God to forgive us, despite the fact that we know we are not worthy, and that we take such comfort in our assurance that, whatever anyone else thinks of us, we are the only ones who truly know how terrible we actually are. By admitting God's power to forgive, we are admitting that the final control over our own lives is not simply ours, but involves others – the other people with whom we live out our relationships, but also, and even more worrying, the creator who knows us better than we know ourselves and whose love makes us into something that our petty power-crazed mind does its very best to shut out.

In the parable above, the two servants are in debt, and the inability to pay that debt results in punishment, in imprisonment and torment. This final aspect is as telling as the premise. Something as simple as bearing a grudge, as feeling superior to another because of a wrong that other has committed, refusing to forgive so as to maintain our hold over another – this obsessive urge to power in our personal relationships is a source, we think, of great security. It keeps us safe. So do the four walls of a prison cell.

There is security that constricts, and security that liberates. Self-assurance, self-protection, smug superiority, however tiny the circumstance, is something that restricts my freedom truly to be the person God made me to be. Refusal to forgive, the storing up of wrongs, is itself an imprisonment which contains the image of God within us, the ability to love and to give of ourselves. Taking the brave step of forgiving our neighbour takes us outside this simple but powerful little world of incarceration and into the great wide open, into the dangerous world of freedom and possibility, the possibility that the love of God can make me something new. And it is that world, the open-air theatre of love and all its risks, that is the world that God created.

So here is the claim of Christianity, that in Jesus Christ we are welcomed into that dangerous new world of unconditional love. But how can this be? Hearing the teaching of Jesus in the Gospel is one thing, claiming that God transforms humanity is something else. As always, we find new ways of thinking and speaking when we look at Jesus Christ. The story of Jesus is the story of self-giving love, and we see this most clearly when we remind ourselves of the climax of Jesus' life, in his execution on the cross and his defeat of death in the new life of Easter.

The love of God we meet in Jesus is the life of God's very self. That life we call the Trinity, and by that word we mean the idea that God in God's self is a perfect community of love. The names we give to God – Father, Son and Holy Spirit – describe something that is always and eternally completely given to the other in love. There is nothing about God that is not given in love, not offered to the other. Selfless love finds its meaning in God, because in the life of God there is literally no self that is not given. Human beings are both like and unlike God, because we are created with the ability to give ourselves in love, and hence to reflect what Scripture called the image of God in human form. It is that love for which we are made, so that the very point of human life is to be like God, to give oneself in love, to offer our lives to God and to our fellow human beings. Unfortunately, where God is self-less, human beings are self-ish. Instead of giving, we take, instead of offering, we keep. Instead of seeing the divine in another we create a false god in ourselves, and make the world conform to a vision of selfish individualism in which love makes no sense and God has no place.

Fortunately for humanity, the love of God is infinitely stronger than our selfishness. God wishes us to exist in loving relationship with him and with others, and seeing us unable to live out that existence, he acts to invite us, to compel us into the divine life in what we call the incarnation, the enfleshment of divine love in the human life of Jesus of Nazareth. The Son of God – the second person of the Trinity – incarnates love by living out the life of God in a single human existence.

Our first chapter began with a story of God's unconditional love. That love, personified in Jesus, confronts the world of self with a life of perfect self-giving. Self-giving that is perfect can hold nothing back, and so the incarnate life of Jesus is also, and inevitably, his death. Jesus must offer his life to the Father, or else he has kept something for himself, he has lived out the selfishness, which it is his mission to overcome. This climax of self-giving is the crucifixion, the death of the Son of God. But this is not an event out of nothing, a new decision on God's part. It is the culmination of everything Jesus has said and done in his mission of divine love. The Son is a sacrifice, something offered and made holy, to the Father because his self-giving on the cross at Golgotha is the earthly consequence of love, the story of God's own life lived in the world that God created. The sacrifice of Christ is the offering of perfect humanity, and that offering transforms all that it means to be human.

Among the many strange claims of Christianity, this one ranks highly. What it means to be human, is transformed by Jesus Christ. This is because God has united humanity and divinity, he has joined humanity to his own life. Humanity is no longer just about being human, it is also about being divine, about sharing in the life of God. Those of us who are human are made to be participants in the divine life through the incarnation of the God who is perfect love. That love now characterizes human beings, despite the fears and failures it provokes. That love, so infinitely beyond anything we can know or understand, reaches beyond our separation, swallows up our distance, and drowns our hatred in the ocean of its embrace. But it does not seem so, of course. Humanity seems as full of death and violence as we can ever imagine, and that seeming is clear when we tell the story of Christ. Encountering the love of God in Jesus, we fall quickly into fear. We are threatened by that love and we cling to our selves and the power we think we retain. This is the response to Jesus of Nazareth. The one who incarnates perfect love becomes not our love but our enemy, something to be opposed and done away with. The fate of love at the hands of fear is the death to which we condemn God himself, to protect ourselves from love and its unsettling consequences.

But this is only part of the story. Love will not be contained by human attempts at power, it will not conform to our assumptions of life and death. The harder we try to make love disappear, the more insistently it mocks our attempts to control it. Jesus, the personification of divine love, is put to death by human violence and buried deep in human darkness. But as our chapter on the resurrection will make clear, nothing human can contain God's perfect love. That love explodes into life, new life, the perfect life of God himself – not the mockery of human insecurity. Human life, in Jesus Christ, is taken from us into God so as to be given to us again, so that what it means to be human is always and forever perfectly offered in the life of God. The divine life – that which brings something from nothing, that which loves things into existence – is now also the life of humanity, and the life of love in humans is now infinitely and eternally possible.

God's forgiveness is God's love made real in our lives, the love we encounter when we meet Jesus Christ. That forgiveness shows itself to us in God's bringing together of earth and heaven, the uniting of our lives with God's. But love, remember, makes no sense. This is not a way of being or of living that will fit into our neatly conceived ideas, or fulfil our desire for a balanced ledger of right and wrong. Instead, in Jesus Christ we find God flooding wrong and failure and absence with love, with the creative goodness which is the life of God himself. This is not an orderly approach to rescuing or redeeming humanity from self and hatred and death. In the past, many Christian thinkers have offered images or models with which we might compare God's action in Christ, and it is easy for us to misunderstand these images as if they were telling us what really happened. They are not, and they cannot, because the infinity of God's love infinitely transcends our powers of description. Instead, they are appealing to our desire to understand, helping us to realize that God's love is not just an idea. We need to recognize that God works within the limitations of the created world to transform it from within, and gives us, in Christ, new ways of thinking and speaking so that we can articulate in part that which goes so far beyond our comprehension.

The cross and resurrection of Christ are basic to this new way of speaking. God turns upside down the most basic of our preconceptions – that death is the opposite of life, and ultimately to be feared – by embracing death and replacing it with unending life. It is no surprise that in the New Testament we read of people describing the early Christians as those who are turning the world upside down.

Music, poetry and art are often more powerful theological media than essays, sermons or books. There is a painting by the Italian artist Caravaggio that expresses powerfully but also simply, the reversal of understanding that the cross of Christ brings about. In English this painting is usually called *The Entombment* and it depicts the lifeless body of Jesus being carried towards burial by Joseph of Arimathea and another disciple (probably meant to be the apostle John), with Mary, the mother of Jesus, Mary Magdalen and another female follower looking on in their grief.

The painting shows a collection of people, five of whom are alive, and one of whom is dead. The dead body is gruesomely realistic as a corpse. But it is also by far the greatest focus of light in the picture, and it contrasts with the dark robe of the apostle John, or the almost mourning dress of the Virgin herself. The arc of the body, which mirrors the strange bent-over arching of Joseph, presents a whirl of light reflected and intensified by the light of the white winding cloth which both mirrors and frames the body. That winding cloth is a shroud, a garment of death, and yet it gleams with an almost clean hope and picks out, in its complex folds, the beautiful ripple of flesh that is the corpse of the Son of God.

At the foot of the picture, forming a foundation, is not a symbol but a fact; the cold stone of the tomb. Jesus' hand rests, gently perhaps, upon this basis. Joseph's feet stand upon it, and so it supports not just him but the body of Jesus and hence the whole composition. The tombstone itself is drawn pointing out towards us, with the apex of the corner marking a central, vertical line as if to point us to the centre of the canvas. The coming together of the corners in that line is the counterpart of that coming together of vertical and horizontal of which Caravaggio is so fond. This convergence outlines the destiny of the viewer's gaze, because the images inexorably point downwards, towards the ground, the flat horizontal of earth. The voice of divinity is silenced, the power of the creator is taken away. What remains is the earth's gift to its God – the impossible death of the source of all life.

In this painting, the world is turned upside down. Life itself is shown to be dead; and yet the death of life itself is the source not of darkness, but of light. The body of Jesus, that which ought to be a symbol of despair, is brilliant with future possibility even as it is being enshrined in the finality of the grave. This picture is a snapshot, a moment in the story. But it is a moment of motion, of action, and the action is burial and entombment. But the consequence of that action is not what one would expect, not the final extinguishing of light but the hope, the new life, that promises to come forth. As the body of Jesus is almost poured into the grave, so the light from his shroud takes us down into the earth and touches a plant, a small tree, a sign of growth. That which is being planted will spring forth in life. The impossibility of life in the corpse of an executed criminal becomes the impossibility of death in the life of God himself.

The New Testament tells us elsewhere that nothing is impossible with God. That little phrase is very telling, 'nothing is impossible'. For nothing, emptiness, the absence of life, is surely what we would expect from the death of God himself. And yet God refuses to conform. Nothing is impossible – that is, our assumptions about death and about nothingness are proved impossible in the suffering, death and burial of Jesus Christ. Rather than welcoming nothingness to rule over our lives and over the world, the death of Christ makes nothingness impossible and brings about the life of the resurrection, which is the subject of our next chapter.

Further Reading

Alison, James (2012), *Knowing Jesus*, London: SPCK.

Groves, Peter (2012), *Grace: The Free, Unconditional and Limitless Love of God*, Norwich: Canterbury Press.

Williams, Rowan (2017), *God With Us*, London: SPCK.

Young, Frances (2016), *Construing the Cross*, London: SPCK.

8

Love Inexhaustible – The Resurrection and Ascension

Jarred Mercer

Resurrection as revelation: recognizing Jesus

The resurrection, which cannot be divorced in our thinking from the ascension, is the foundation of knowing Jesus. This is our starting place – not Genesis, or the prophets, or the Law, or even Christ's incarnation. The resurrection is the source of our faith. All of these other aspects of our story only begin to come into view when the light of the resurrection breaks upon them. The resurrection is the context of it all: of who Jesus really is, of who God is and who we are, and of the senselessness of God's love for us.

You may remember that in the story of Jesus in the Gospels no one got it! Not even his closest friends and followers (John 20.9; 2.22; 12.16; Luke 9.45; 18.34; Mark 9.32). No one saw who Jesus really was. They all, *we* all, sit in darkness until the light of Easter morning bursts out of the tomb. Mary Magdalen recognizes Jesus by hearing him say her name (John 20.16); John recognizes Jesus when he sees the abandoned linen cloths where he once lay dead (John 20.8); Thomas recognizes Jesus by touching his wounds (John 20.27–28); the two disciples on the road to Emmaus recognize Jesus through tasting eucharistic bread (Luke 24.35); and the disciples collectively recognize him in his breath (John 20.22), his touch (Luke 24.39) and, of all things, breakfast and dinner (John 20.10–14; Luke 24.42). But they all recognized Jesus, the fullness of who Jesus is, only after encountering him as resurrected.

This is why the rest of the New Testament affirms that the resurrection-ascension of Christ is the very heart of the Christian faith. For the apostle Paul, Christ's resurrection (and our participation in it) is really just what the Christian faith is: belief in Jesus is belief in Jesus resurrected (Rom. 1.4; 1 Cor. 15.3–4). Faith in God is faith in the God of the resurrection (1 Cor. 15.15). To be a person of this faith, a Christian, is to be the people of the resurrection who share in Christ's risen life (Phil. 3.10–11; 1 Cor. 6.14; 1 Thess. 4.14; Rom. 8.11; 2 Cor. 4.14). Paul goes as far as to say that our faith is vain and we are, above all, people most to be pitied if there is no resurrection (1 Cor. 15.12–19).

Furthermore, the resurrection-ascension does not only lay the foundation for our faith, but opens us up to the rest of Christian theology. We recognize Jesus to be the Lord of all through the resurrection-ascension (Phil. 2.8–11). We only know Jesus as truly the Son of God through the resurrection-ascension (Rom. 1.4), and we receive the gift of the Holy Spirit through the resurrection-ascension (John 7.39; 16.7). And through it we know ourselves to be Christ's body, the Church, the community of new creation (Rom. 8.29; 2 Cor. 5.17; 1 Cor. 15.20–23). In other words, what we call Christology (the study of Christ), the doctrine of the Trinity, of the Church (ecclesiology), of our salvation (soteriology), and the doctrine of creation, all rest on the resurrection of Jesus. Without Jesus' resurrection from the dead, we do not know Jesus truly *as* Jesus, or God truly as Christians believe God to be, or even ourselves as we are and as we are meant to be.

God is the God of resurrection. Jesus is the resurrection. We are the people of the resurrection. This is the heart of our faith because it is simply who we say God is and who we believe ourselves to be. Christians do not make sense – we do not exist – outside the resurrection life of Jesus Christ. Scripture continually points us to this baseline source of knowing and loving God. Resurrection is revelation – both of who God is and of who we are. And this revelation is the foundation of faith in God through Jesus Christ.

Thomas did not want to touch the wounds of Jesus in order to acquire intellectually whether or not the resurrection was real. ('Let's see, who was right, the Pharisees who believe in resurrection or the Sadducees who do not?') He wanted to know who his Lord and God truly was. The resurrection is the foundation of our faith not because it gives us some fundamental idea or fact about Christianity to build upon, but because it reveals to us who this Jesus really is. And knowing Jesus, really knowing Jesus, is what faith is all about. We are not after cognitive assent, but true and loving knowledge of Jesus as Lord, Saviour and friend.

In learning and living the resurrection we are learning who Christ truly is and who we truly are. When we look then at Christ and ourselves through the lens of the resurrection, who do we discover Christ to be? And what do we learn about ourselves?

Resurrection as life: entering the new creation
At the heart of the identity of Jesus Christ is that he is the crucified

and risen one. Note, he is not the *once* crucified and *then* risen one, as if the crucifixion and resurrection shared some sort of prelude-postlude or cause and effect relationship. Too often in contemporary Christianity, theologians and preachers have focused only on the cross as the point of salvation, almost entirely without reference to the resurrection. The cross is seen as the point of our redemption and the resurrection the necessary 'next step'.

But the resurrection is not an afterthought; it is not something that depends upon the crucifixion. It is not as if God thought, 'Oh, no! Christ has died. I must do something about that'. To put it less crudely, it is not as though God foresaw the crucifixion and therefore planned the resurrection as a solution to clean up the mess and fix the problem of Christ's execution.

The cross is a problem, of course. It is evil. This is, while part of the 'good news', or gospel, nonetheless very bad news about *us*. This is senseless, pointless, heinous, gratuitous evil, as this innocent victim, this pure victim – one who has always and only ever been a victim and never made victims out of others – is brutally murdered in public shame. It's an extraordinary and we would say unbelievable picture of our rejection of love (that is, sin)- if we did not know how easy it is for us humans to create victims, how skilled we are at scapegoating others to save ourselves It is what Christians have called the summary of all human sin.

Yes, this is a problem of biblical proportions, as they say, but the resurrection is not just some solution. It is not reactionary or secondary. It is actually primary. Life, creation, is primary, not reactionary to death and destruction, so the resurrected Christ is the inevitable conclusion, the only possible reality of Christ crucified.

Christians call Jesus God. We claim that he is divine. The infinite divine life, the perfect life, power, and love of God are present in this human Jesus. When we look at the life of Jesus we witness what it looks like for God to live among us. God is always and everywhere creative – everything that God touches comes alive. And the cross is no different. When touched, even entered into, by the unconquerable and unending life of God, even death has no choice but to come alive. Indeed, death in Christ not only comes to life, but becomes life-giving. The resurrection means Christ's death is creative.

One thing that Scripture emphasizes concerning the unified work of the crucifixion and resurrection for our salvation is the picture of Christ's identity stated above: Christ is the crucified and risen one. Christ was not just once crucified and then re-surrected. He is what James Alison calls the 'living dead' (Alison, 1993, p. 20). The resurrection is not on a par with death (remember, life, not death, is primary), cancelling it out, or again, 'solving the problem'. This is not just a resuscitation back to life as it was, as if Jesus died at the age of 33 and rose at the age of 33 plus a few more days. The whole divine and human life is gifted back to Jesus, and to us, in the resurrection. Christ is always now present as the crucified one, and Christ is always now present as the risen and ascended one. In the resurrection, everything that it means to be a human being, to know God and be in relationship to and with God – to bleed, to die, to suffer, to be broken and to be restored in new life, love and joy – is re-created, re-established, and breathed into a new existence.

But life does not come from death. It's impossible. Victory is not found in defeat in the world as we know it. This is a complete mockery of the world order. The whole world is turned on its head, and we come undone and are remade. Resurrection is new creation.

One important aspect to remember about this is that the risen and ascended Jesus is *human*. Jesus was not more human before the crucifixion and more divine after resurrection, or a different sort of human than he was previously, or than we are, after the resurrection. The Christ who rose is the crucified Christ. Our very human condition, the same humanity that Christ inhabited throughout his life, is brought into the glory of God, enters the new creation, reigns from heaven with God in Christ. Normal, everyday humanity – wounded, bruised, scarred – is restored and renewed in resurrection life. This has at least two very significant implications for us. One is that we, the real you and me with all our faults and frailties and insecurities and wounds, are welcomed into the new life of resurrection in Christ. Our humanity is carried through to redemption and glory through Christ, so that we share in his resurrection life.

Our destiny is altered, or in a way recovered, through Christ's life, death and resurrection-ascension. We were not made for death. Death is normal in that it happens to all of us, but it is not *normative*; it is not really natural to who we are and who we were created to be – the whole point of creation is that something might exist, not that something that exists might cease to exist! We were meant for life, not death, and so Christ enters into that unnatural state of death, reaches into it, and turns it towards life in order to restore us to our true nature. And so the resurrection is the institution of the new creation. Our human nature is re-created by entering into a life that cannot die, one that has passed through death and conquered it. We are, in the death of Christ, restored to life. Resurrection is life.

The second implication of the humanness of Christ's resurrection is that it is a resurrection *of the body*.

Resurrection as redemption: the embodiment of forgiveness

Athanasius, one of the most important theologians of the early Church, wrote: 'The supreme object of his coming was to bring about the resurrection of the body' (*On the Incarnation*, 4.22). The supreme object? Didn't Jesus come to save us from our sins? To redeem the world? Precisely. The distinctive and central Christian belief of the resurrection of the body is salvation, forgiveness – the redemption of the world. Resurrection is redemption.

Christianity has been called the religion of the incarnation (from the Latin *incarnari*, 'to be made flesh'). We are the people of God enfleshed, God embodied. The body matters to us. And we only know Jesus as embodied. Christ exists, Christ lives, as bodily risen and not otherwise, and we too only exist as our bodies. We are created by God as bodily beings. As Thomas Aquinas once said: 'My soul is not me.' As the chapter on the incarnation in this book makes clear, this is at the very heart of our faith. God is not a God who is far off and distant, some grandfather figure floating around in the sky. God shows up. God makes God's self known in the real, ordinary, mundane reality of our lives. And this is necessary for us to know who God is and what God is like. We cannot know as dogs, or trees, or stars, or as merely spirits or souls; we know and experience and love and desire and need and want only as embodied humans. And so that is exactly where God meets us. A non-bodily resurrection would be one that ceases to be human and one that is no good to us at all, and one that we ourselves could never know or experience.

The resurrection of the body has numerous implications for Christian life (and indeed, human life generally). It means first that God cares. God does not only love some ethereal idea of us divorced from our everyday life and existence, from who we really are. Nor does God love only the nice or pretty bits of us. As Christ brings every aspect of human life through death and into God's loving embrace, a declaration is made to each one of us: 'every aspect of who you are is the object of my love and affection and care. I love all of you, every part of you. All of it is embraced in my reckless and extravagant love.' In the resurrection, the whole of Christ's existence is given back to him, every part of human life, and so the resurrection is the creation of a new bodily, material world, a 'glorified' world as Paul has it (1 Cor. 15.42–53), the new way of being human.

This transforms our life and world even now as we are shaped towards that destiny. In Christ, we are who we are becoming. This is, again, because the resurrection does not just show or teach us something about the salvation of the world. It *is* that salvation. It *is* new and eternal life. The resurrection does not just open doors for us to forgiveness, for instance. It is not a statement of forgiveness, or merely the offering of forgiveness, it is forgiveness embodied and present in a human being. Resurrection is forgiveness.

Jesus is a particular person, not a generalized 'humanity'. When his life is given back anew it is a life with a particular history, a life of particular memories. It is a life that can call Mary Magdalen by name, that can meet Peter on the beach, that has friends to embrace. It is a life with past wounds that can be touched and seen; a life broken and restored. Jesus resurrected is the living presence of God's gratuitous and overwhelming forgiveness – a forgiveness that restores our personal wounds, that breathes new life into our particular relationships, that welcomes every single part of each one of us into renewal and fulfilment.

Jesus' encounter with Peter on the beach after his resurrection is the perfect example of this (John 21.15–17). Jesus questions whether Peter loves him three times, just as Peter had denied Christ three times before his death. He stands before Peter as forgiveness, as hope realized, as Peter's restoration – handing Peter back his history of sin and brokenness transformed into love. And this love awakens Peter to a new forgiven life, with a mission to love others, as Jesus charges him to 'feed my sheep'.

The resurrection embodies our forgiveness and hope. It is the restoration of our histories into timeless, perfect love.

Resurrection as love: the gift of the body

This embodiment of our salvation makes itself present continually in the world through Christ's love alive in the Church. This is a further result of the resurrection of the body. We are the community of the Lord who reigns, risen and ascended. The community of the resurrection. To live under the reign of the resurrected one is to live his resurrected life in the world; that life of love, forgiveness, restoration and wholeness. Christ did not give us a moral code, a way of life through instruction for us to follow. He gifted himself to us. So when we speak of living the Christian faith, of theology as a lived, practised, reality, we are simply talking about living 'in Christ', about being Christ's body, the Church. Christ himself is the resurrection and the life, and as the people of his kingdom we are called to live in that life.

This life, this grace and love, is not abstract. It is gifted to us in the real, earthy, bodily, life of Christ. When we are brought into this life, when we are 'united with him in resurrection' (Rom. 6.5), we too through the Spirit offer this love and life to others. The community of the resurrection of which Christ is the 'first fruits' is a community of gift. To be a Christian is to be a part of that broken and restored, wound-bearing, scarred body, and it is to carry that body into and for the world now, for its own healing and restoration.

The resurrection then is not only our future hope but also the road to that hope. It is the life we lead now. The self-giving love of Christ that is made present in our world through his death and resurrection is now ours, Christ's community of gift to offer to the world. Christ in his death and bodily resurrection brings the wounded and broken in the world through to redemption. This is what salvation looks like. Christ throughout his life shows us that he is on the side of the poor and neglected, the suffering and the wounded and, in his death and resurrection, he becomes the wounded and suffering one, the neglected, the poor. This is hope and redemption for the most vulnerable and oppressed people of our world, and it also shows us where God's love goes. Jesus is the perfect love of God embodied in a human being, and when divine love shows up on the human stage, it finds itself with the broken and outcasts. It finds itself, indeed, as the world's saving victim. Resurrection is love.

Living the resurrection is living a life on offer as a gift of love to those the world has rejected. The risen body of Christ alive in the world today is a body that is thrown into the world's suffering, seeking to bring healing and renewal. This is what makes sense of Christ's radical teaching in Matthew 25, where at the last judgement he turns to those on one side and welcomes them into his kingdom because when he was hungry they fed him, when he was thirsty they gave him drink, they visited him when he was in prison and clothed him when he was naked, saying that whenever they did these things for those who are 'least' in the world, they actually did them for him. He then turns to those on the other side. They are those who were preachers and evangelists, those who taught Sunday school and small group Bible studies, and those who kept all the rules, and he tells them that he does not know them because they neglected the 'least' around them, and in doing so neglected to love and serve him. Jesus is the victim of the world, of each one of us, and it is in the world's victims today that we meet him face to face.

The life of the resurrection, the life of our faith, is not about having the right answers, or proving that Jesus' tomb is empty, it is a life of self-giving love – a life embodying the love of Jesus Christ. The starving bodies of the hungry are meant to feast for eternity at the table of the Lord. The lost and lonely bodies of refugees are meant for their eternal welcome. The bypassed bodies of those experiencing homelessness are eternal, and have an eternal home. Minority bodies discriminated against are made for eternal belonging. This is why the view that some Christians express that 'saving souls' is all that matters is, quite frankly, distinctly unchristian. The idea that getting people to think or believe like us about certain theological principles or propositions is the aim of Christian mission rather than the renewal of all things is to ignore the resurrection of Jesus Christ (the source of our faith). It is just not possible to live an authentic Christian life without seeking to feed and house those who are poor, welcoming the outcast (whether or not they agree with us!), befriending sinners (whether or not they stop sinning!). Nor is it possible to think that our Christianity (that is, our sharing in Christ's re-surrection life) can be divorced from the political realm, from issues of healthcare, education, war, immigration and welcome of the stranger, the environment, and so on. The Christian faith, resurrection faith, is holistic, encompassing every aspect of our lives.

The incarnate, crucified, risen and ascended Jesus proclaims that bodies matter, that this world matters. He says that he came to renew all things, not to save 'souls' and leave bodies behind – which is much more akin to something we call gnosticism than it is Christianity. Christians who separate care for the vulnerable and outcasts, the poor and neglected from Christian life or the mission of the Church are denying the Christian doctrine of the resurrection with their lives if not their words. Indeed, even rejecting Christ himself, who is the poor, the vulnerable, the outcast – the victim of us all.

This is not to de-emphasize evangelism or the proclamation of the gospel. It is just to say that the gospel is bigger than words about Jesus, as he himself makes clear (remember Matthew 25). The resurrection of the body shows that Christ's salvation is holistic and is about whole lives and our whole world, so that sharing in Christ's resurrection life and mission must also be holistic.

Resurrection as hope: discerning the body

The Eucharist is at the centre of this. As the disciples at Emmaus recognized Jesus in the breaking of the bread (Luke 24.35), so do we meet Christ in the Eucharist today, where we share in the broken, resurrected and ascended body of Christ. The Eucharist is the continual presence of the crucified and risen Lord among us. It is the making present of Christ's crucifixion and resurrection in our lives today. In the Eucharist, we are offered up and given back anew – given resurrection life – as we remember, as our particular history is brought into contact, into dialogue, with the cross and resurrection of Jesus. As the particular history of Jesus is brought through death into resurrection, as Peter is given back his true self by the resurrected Christ on the beach, so in the

Eucharist we bring our whole selves, our unique individual and corporate histories to Christ crucified and risen. We recall our history of betrayal, of sin, of our 'old humanity' (Col. 3.9–10; Rom. 6.6; 1 Pet. 2.24), of our participation in Christ's victimization at the cross and, through feasting on the essence and source of our life, we are united as his body, we are 'resurrected', given ourselves back anew after dying to sin and overcoming death in Christ. And all of it, all of it is renewed, transfigured and returned to us as gift. Resurrection is restoration.

This is why Christians from the very beginning have spoken of the Eucharist as a share in Christ's resurrection, from Ignatius of Antioch (*Epistle to the Ephesians*, 20) and Irenaeus (*Against Heresies*, IV.18.5; V.2.2–3) among the earliest generations of Jesus' followers, to Jesus himself: 'Those who eat my flesh and drink my blood have eternal life, and I will raise them up on the last day' (John 6.54). Eternal life, resurrection, is explicitly tied to the eucharistic feast. This is because the Eucharist unites us with the events of Christ's crucifixion and resurrection: we find ourselves with him in the garden, in the upper room, at the foot of the cross, and rejoicing at the empty tomb. But it is also because of the incarnational, embodied nature of Christianity. Christ meets us in the real world. God's perfect love inhabits human life and reality, and in resurrection – in that bodily, material reality in which what it means to be a human being is not abandoned, but renewed and transformed – God's perfect love continues to meet us where we are in the real world: the fruit of the vine; the work of human hands.

But the Eucharist makes the risen Christ present in our lives and world in an even fuller sense as we begin to meet Christ in one another. We not only recognize the broken and restored body of Christ in bread and wine but in Christ's body, the Church. Not only are basic elements of human nourishment transformed for our spiritual nourishment, making Christ present to us, but Christ's transfigured body, ascended and reigning over all, is united to the Christian community, making Christ present the whole world over. We become the community of resurrection, where forgiveness, mercy and love are found; where victims are restored, and the marginalized and rejected are welcomed. Through the Eucharist, the resurrection life of Christ on offer for the world is lived out in us.

This is why Scripture marries the formation of the eucharistic community with the liberation of the oppressed and care for all in need. Paul chastises the church in Corinth who welcomed Christ among them in the sacrament, but excluded the poor and hungry from their tables (1 Cor. 11.17–34). As Gerald O'Collins points out (O'Collins, 2013), Paul's words that they partook of the Eucharist 'without discerning the body' (v. 29) have two meanings. We can fail to perceive Christ as present among us in the sacrament, our spiritual food, but also fail to discern Christ present among us in those with nothing to eat.

Jesus himself makes this connection as his words at the Last Supper, the institution of the Eucharist, 'Take and eat' (Matt. 26.26), are directly linked to the words of the previous chapter of Matthew's Gospel, 'I was hungry and you gave me food' (Matt. 25.35). The risen Jesus is the same Jesus with the same particular history, who ate with prostitutes, sinners and tax collectors and spent his life with the poorest in his society. He is the same Jesus who gave himself for them – and for the forgiveness of their own histories – on the cross, and who continually offers his broken body for the nourishment of their own brokenness, 'transforming their alienation into companionship' (O'Collins, p. 159). To feed on Christ and be nourished in the Eucharist only to neglect to offer oneself and one's resources as food for others is to refuse to live out the resurrection faith we confess.

While the coming of Christ's kingdom is a work of grace that does not depend upon human action, we cannot separate the hope of the kingdom with hope present in the world now. We are to live as a foretaste of that kingdom and as agents of hope in the midst of the world's despair. We do not only speak about lives of reconciliation but we live them: the forgiven life, the restored life, the life of hope. Resurrection is hope.

We declare our belief in the resurrection not by stating it as a fact of our faith, and not only by proclaiming it, but by inhabiting the space in the world that the risen Christ inhabits, by abiding where Christ abides – in the community of his risen body and in the midst of the poor and broken.

The ascension: hope realized

I opened this chapter by saying that the resurrection and ascension belong together. Indeed, Scripture often makes no real distinction between them at all. Matthew's account is simply that the risen Christ reigns, and similarly for Mark the risen Christ is the glorified Christ. Luke's Gospel account makes no distinction between the two (though Luke has a separate account of the ascension in Acts), and John's Gospel also has no separate ascension account. There is a theological distinction to be made, but not one that removes the inherent connection of the two events. They are of one progression, one journey in the same story. The ascension brings about Christ's promise to his disciples that he will be with them always (Matt. 28.20), but the risen Christ is in a sense already the ascended Christ, already received into glory and already establishing his kingdom and reign (Matt. 28.18).

When we begin to talk about the ascension, we cannot let go of this connection, and not just the connection with the risen Christ, but with his whole life, death, resurrection and coming again. Focusing in on the ascension apart from the entire narrative of Christ's existence distorts its meaning and leaves us bewildered (in the same way the resurrection makes no sense without crucifixion and vice versa).

Jesus is always 'going to the Father' (John 16.5, 10, 17, 28; 20.17). The ascension is not a novelty: 'I will be with you a little while longer, and then I am going to him who sent me' (John 7.33). There is a continual movement of Christ towards the Father. And this is more or less the point. God comes to us in Christ. God shows up among us: God's perfect love and life abiding in human life. But that is only one side of it. The gospel is not just the coming of Christ, and it is not just the crucifixion, or even the crucifixion and resurrection, it is the entire motion of 'God-with-us': Emmanuel. God the Son assumes humanity in Christ, carries that humanity through the perfect life it was meant to live, takes the 'old humanity' down into the grave and brings it through to resurrection life. And in the ascension Christ finally carries our human condition with him into glory.

This full movement of Christ's life is what allows Jesus not only to be always 'going to the Father', but to be going to the Father *with us*: 'and where I am, there will my servant be also' (John 12.26); 'Where I am, there you may be also' (John 14.3); 'Father, I desire that those also, whom you have given me, may be with me where I am, to see my glory' (John 17.24).

The ascension is not a zapping of Jesus back up to the mother ship, and is certainly not an escape from humanity or the worldly, earthy, bodily existence that Jesus shares with us. The ascension is simply the completion of the first movement of the incarnation.

As in the incarnation divinity was introduced into human life, so in the ascension humanity is introduced into the divine life. The human condition now inhabits heaven, the eternal presence of God. In Christ, humanity forever now exists as present with God in infinite love. The ascension is the realization of our salvation: humanity has been exalted to enjoy the perfect love of God. Ascension is hope realized.

The gospel is not a one-sided movement of God to us, but a double-sided movement which through the humility of God brings humble creatures into the glory of God's love. God's life with us in Jesus Christ involves both descent, beginning with the manger and culminating in the cross, and ascent. As the cross shows God's enacted love to be unbounded and indiscriminate, penetrating even into the darkest points of our existence, so the resurrection and ascension show God's love to be inexhaustible. It is a love that cannot be defeated, even in death. It is a love without end. And it is a love gifted to us.

This means that just as Jesus was 'going to the Father', so we are headed somewhere. It means that our weakness, our frailty, our brokenness, our sin and shame, are manifestly not the truest things about us. Christ shows us that we have a different, and gloriously different, future. And this future, this hope, is already accomplished, already realized in Christ so that in him, as his 'body', we are journeying towards our true home.

Further Reading

Alison, James (2003), *On Being Liked*, London: Darton, Longman & Todd.

McGrath, Alister (2007), *Resurrection*, London: SPCK.

Williams, Rowan (2017), *God With Us: The Meaning of the Cross and Resurrection – Then and Now*, London: SPCK.

Williams, Rowan (2014; originally published 1982), *Resurrection: Interpreting the Easter Gospel*, London: Darton, Longman & Todd.

9

Love Entrusted – The Sacraments

Melanie Marshall

Pledges of love

How do you know that you are loved?

On placement in the north of England, I addressed a primary school assembly with this question. First I checked that the children each had someone who loved them and received eager confirmation. Then I asked them: how do you know? Every hand flew up and examples poured out, each more touching than the last. But the one who stuck in my mind was a little girl whose answer was this: that when she wanted a drink of water and was too short to reach the tap, her auntie poured it for her. Love, in a cup of cold water.

Or in a little piece of bread or a smear of oil or the touch of a hand. The answers the children gave were very like the answer the Church gives. Small actions, often repeated, taking place in the context of a relationship; actions that both create that relationship and strengthen it – these are how we know that we are loved. Anyone who has had a friend or been part of a family understands this. Through Jesus Christ, God has made a new family, cobbled together by joining all kinds of people to Christ's body and decreeing that they are one body and one family. This family, the Church, is created and strengthened by habitual gestures, which are given the name 'sacraments' (this comes from the Latin word *sacramentum*, meaning an oath or pledge of consecration to the gods). The Church is no different from any other family in that way. Nonetheless it is a big family spread all across the world and its practices have continued and evolved over 20 centuries. Because of this, these gestures have generated a lot of conversation and various conventions have grown up around them. This chapter talks about how sacraments are performed and understood by the Church. But we must never lose sight of the fact that they are, above all, simple pledges of love.

The greatest pledge of love ever known is the person Jesus of Nazareth. Like other pledges of love, Jesus emerges in the context of a relationship, the relationship between God and humankind. God made the world, including us. All that we need to grow in health and joy has simply been given us without price. So, for the faithful, the whole of creation is a tangible pledge or sign that God is there and loves us – what one Orthodox theologian has called 'the world as sacrament'. However, humans have not shown themselves adept at receiving the whole world as a God-soaked gift. God knows this and is always helping his people with pledges of divine love. Look in the Old Testament and you will see prophets, saving acts, priests, sacrifice, teachers. Jesus is yet another pledge, but of a quite different order. He is God himself, present among us as a man. As a human being, Jesus shows us how we should receive divine love. He models perfect gratitude and disinterested delight in everything God has made (as Adam should have done, and didn't). But as God, Jesus' life also shows us how active divine love is. It restores, cleanses, nourishes, reconciles, encourages, admonishes, soothes and directs, to name but a few of the things Jesus does in the Gospels. It even does things that we normally consider impossible. In his earthly life Jesus transformed people, partly by the things he said but just as importantly by the things he did.

Jesus, then, is the first sacrament. He is a tangible sign of God's love. He is a sign that is not just there to be interpreted passively, like a road sign. He is also active, a sign that forges or strengthens the love-bond that it signifies, like an embrace. In Jesus, God takes something that was already there, something everyday and widespread (that is, human existence), and suffuses it with divine presence and power. God does this in a bodily form because we are bodily, and can only learn through our bodies, through what we see and hear and touch. Christians are people who have touched God (1 John 1.1), and people whom God has touched. Christians go on using physical acts and objects as ways of transmitting that divine touch from Christian to Christian over every generation.

The opportunity to touch the earthly Jesus has gone. It passed when he died 2,000 years ago. However, Jesus was given a trans-formed body when he rose from the dead. It is not like a mortal human body. It is much more real and substantial, because it is a physical manifestation of the reality and eternity of God's very self. This means it is not easy to describe. Even Jesus' closest friends couldn't recognize it without help. But this body is not meant to be described. St Paul follows the prophet Isaiah when he says that no eye has seen, nor ear heard, nor mind imagined, the future that is signified by that body (1 Cor. 2.9). Christ's resurrection body is not an object in the world, then, but a promise: that the life of God can one day be ours. That risen and eternal body of Jesus, and so that promise, is present each time a sacrament takes place. Every sacrament is a meeting with the resurrected Jesus.

How do sacraments come about?

Sacraments are as wondrous as Jesus stilling a storm with a single word. They are also as ordinary as the sun rising to light us from our beds. The whole of creation is an astounding miracle, as the great theologian St Augustine observed. By what rationale does the Church single out certain actions and say that these, and not others, carry special significance for showing us God's love?

One answer is that the sacraments of the Church begin with actions Jesus himself performed. In the Gospels of Mark and Matthew, the first act of Jesus' public ministry is to call people to repentance. From this, the Church derives the sacrament of *reconciliation*. Jesus himself underwent *baptism* and commanded us to baptize in the name of the Trinity, and he blessed a *marriage* with a divine miracle of abundance. The night before he died Jesus taught his closest followers to celebrate the feast of the *Eucharist* in his memory. He also washed their feet, and sent them out to spread the gospel, and these forms of commissioning are reflected in *confirmation* and *ordination*. There is no record of him using oil, but he healed many people with his touch, which continues in the sacrament of *unction*. With varying emphases, Jesus could be said to have instituted all the sacraments while on earth.

This is not a perfect answer. There are only seven sacraments and Jesus did more than seven wonderful things when he was among us in his earthly body. He himself enjoyed more than seven kinds of ministry. Still, these parallels remind us that there is a connection, and not an arbitrary one, between the Lord's own earthly life and the special actions where we can be sure of meeting him today. Remember too that the Church is not a neat development, formed on rigid lines ruled straight between the Gospels and today's world. It is a human family formed out of loving response to God's love for us. Its enduring customs reflect the enduring needs of its members. The miracle of birth and peril of death; the consecration of a life to the particular duties of marriage or religion; the moment of adult commitment and the urgent need for intimation of God's forgiveness; and the unity of the weekly family banquet. The actions we honour as sacraments mark those moments when we most long for a sign of God's presence and blessing.

Some reformed Christians count only two sacraments because the Lord institutes only baptism and the Eucharist explicitly. All Christians regard these as the two most important. Jesus himself flags them up as the crucial ways of participating in his divine life (John 6.53; Mark 16.16; see also 1 Pet. 3.21). However, this is not to dismiss the others as unnecessary. Healing and reconciliation are specific to pastoral need, but most Christians would be helped by them at one point or another. Marriage and ordination are sacraments that only some individuals should take up personally, but all members of the Church benefit from them. Seven has been the definitive number for the last seven centuries or so, and seems settled for now. The Medieval Christians who counted as many as 30 sacraments must have seen the world as very God-soaked indeed, not to mention having very tired priests. The Church performs various actions – exorcism, consecrating people to the religious life, blessing things – and we do not need to call them all sacraments to recognize them as fine and godly functions. God is with us in all the licit actions of his Church, and beyond.

Sacraments and transformation

Sacraments transform things. They transform material substances. They transform human customs. They transform people's lives. These are different kinds of transformation, but they depend on one another. For Christians, God is at work in the whole of creation, from molecules to heartbreaks. The special signs of God's love are full of God's action at every level.

I

In creation God causes the universe to exist out of nothing. In sacraments God takes something that is already in creation and makes it into something different. They are both miraculous deeds that only God can do. But they are not quite the same. Sacraments do not add to creation. They hallow what God has already made and blessed, and they set it aside for a special purpose. In baptism, ordinary water becomes holy water when the Church's prescribed words and actions are used. In the Eucharist, normal bread and wine become the body and blood of Jesus. In unction, cooking oil becomes the sign of divine healing. Using Château d'Yquem or water from the Jordan or extra-virgin olive oil is pointless and a mistake. Nor can you diminish a sacrament by using the cheapest oil or the nastiest plonk. It is not our tastes but God's action that changes this ordinary material into a vessel of divine love. Of course, God's action is always mediated. In sacraments this happens through God's Church and its ministers. These too may vary in quality, whether of expertise or moral fibre. That makes no difference either. Assuming only that the main words and actions are right, those alone guarantee the sacrament, not the priest's eyesight or purity of heart. God's will and the faith of the Church make up any little (and some big) shortfalls.

Still, a lot of ink is spilt on how sacraments do their transforming work. How do the bishop's hands on my head transmit the Holy Spirit in confirmation? How do words spoken and rings exchanged turn a romance into a marriage? Most controversial of all, how do a priest's words and gestures make the glorified body of Jesus physically present in the Eucharist? These questions are perennial, and great ill-feeling has been caused in the Church by the claims of some parties to have exclusive answers. Sacraments are not magic tricks or chemistry lessons. They are an operation of the Holy Spirit. You may as well ask how Sophie and Dominic, for example, know they love each other, or how God became a man in Jesus Christ, or how the saints are in glory. They are interesting questions and we are sure to ask them, but no one would offer or accept a purely mechanistic answer. Like sacraments, these are mysteries, revelations of divine love that human reason can apprehend to an extent but can never exhaust. We are called to enter into mysteries and to allow them to examine and make sense of us, not the other way round. We may take an interest in the various theories, but we shouldn't mistake them for an explanation of what is, praise God, inexplicable. Love makes no sense, remember?

2

A second kind of sacramental transformation takes place when an existing institution is changed into a Christian sacrament. This may surprise some people. We tend to think of the sacraments (except marriage) as activities with no existence outside the Church at all. Yet all these activities have parallels and precedents outside the Church. Baptism and other forms of ritual bathing existed long before Jesus. But everything that Jesus touches, he transforms. So when Jesus undergoes John's baptism (Matt. 3.13–17), baptism itself is changed. It is no longer only for the forgiveness of sins; it becomes a sign of his coming death and resurrection as well. Christians are then baptized into Jesus' life, death and resurrection and it becomes our own. In a similar way, the Eucharist transforms the existing Passover meal. It remains the unifying family meal of God's people. But by God's people we now mean all those for whom Christ died, and the food is not a sacrificed animal but God's own body and the eternal life it offers.

All the sacraments follow this pattern. Anointing for healing and election is found in the Old Testament and across the ancient Mediterranean. The gesture is changed for ever after God in Christ has used his own hands to cure disease and spiritual sickness, and has himself received anointing before his death (John 12.3). It becomes a sign that God is taking a sick person in and giving them new life, whether here on earth or in heaven. Oil is also used for ordination and confirmation (and coronation for that matter). There too it is a sign of appropriation. We are God's and God will keep and direct us in all we do. This direction is something else transformed by Jesus. God had chosen many prophets, priests, judges and kings to guide people in the past and goes on doing so. But Christ sublimes all these figures by showing perfect obedience to God's will in every detail. When Christians accept confirmation or ordination, we are not only agreeing to listen to God's word and follow God's chosen guides. We are promising to be as Christ himself was: obedient to the point of death.

Likewise, followers of all ancient religions were concerned with establishing a right relationship between God (or the gods) and humankind. The usual way of achieving this was the ritual sacrifice of animals or other natural commodities. But once God is united to humanity and humanity is united to God, reconciliation can no longer be a transaction, like sacrificing a goat. Jesus himself is our reconciliation. This is the force of all of Paul's letters. Christ's willing sacrifice of himself on the cross exceeds and includes all the offerings that anyone else could ever make (Heb. 10.10–14). In the sacrament of reconciliation (sometimes called confession), Christians remember that we cannot earn, bargain or implore forgiveness. We can only receive it as a freely offered gift.

Marriage is the sacrament with the longest history outside the Church. Marriage customs vary according to the cultural and theological conventions of a nation or of individual couples, and even in predominantly Christian countries Christian marriage is no longer the only or most usual form. In England the option to be married by a priest still attracts many people who are not otherwise practising Christians. But none of this should blind us to the existence of a distinctive Christian sacrament of marriage. Like the other sacraments it is a human custom that has been transformed by Christ. Historically, marriage aimed to safeguard the transmission of property, the production of legal heirs, and the protection of women and children from desertion. The fidelity of the sexual bond was the pledge of this agreement. Whatever personal meaning couples have given their own marriages, that is the basic form of the worldwide practice.

But Christ blessed a wedding with his presence and with a miracle of abundant fine wine (John 2.1–12). God meant the marriage to bring more and richer joy than the human couple and their guests could imagine or supply. For Christians the pledge to stay together is a sign of the love of God who will never leave us or forsake us. Their home is there to be shared when others need stability. It may provide for the growth of new human lives (and, we hope, Christian disciples), but Christian marriage always affirms that the promise of our immortality comes from Jesus alone and not from offspring who may or may not outlive us. Exclusive sexual intimacy is meant to promote spiritual friendship and not property rights. Many kinds of desire masquerade under the name of love, especially love between couples. The sacrament of marriage invites couples to let Christ be present and transform all their desires into true self-giving.

3

Sacraments transform materials and institutions, but their meaning and purpose is to transform people. Marriage is one example. The desire for partnership is common and natural (though not universal). Christ bestows his grace and perfects the longings nature has bestowed. Daily life is transformed for a married couple. Their lives and habits become unrecognizable, so full are they of concern for the other and not themselves. So it is with all the sacraments. God gives us our deepest desires. And he gives us concrete ways to live out those desires, so they can be turned to his glory and his people's help.

Bishops, priests and deacons provide another example of how transformative a sacrament can be. Those in holy orders vow to undertake special duties within the Church and community. They often live in designated housing and wear distinctive clothing. They subsist on a fixed stipend and are discouraged from earning money. They use different titles and sometimes take different names. (Much of this is also true of monks, friars and nuns.) They are called to new and surprising places of need. Bishops and priests become the ordinary ministers of all the other sacraments, holding the Church together. The sacrament of orders takes a basic desire – to serve – and transforms a person into a lifelong servant of the servants of God.

These transformations of holy matrimony and holy orders come with clear social markers. In other sacraments the transformation is not publicly signalled. We do not wear golden rings to show we have been to confession or adopt special collars when we have been anointed. However, the changes are every bit as real and lasting. They too stem from deep desires. Reconciliation is an object of longing throughout the Scriptures. To be separated from God is death. To be at peace with God and other people is life. Yet, as Chapter 6 on sin and suffering explores more fully, we persist in doing things that harm these relationships and often feel unable to stop. God gives us the desire to come back to him, and in the sacrament of reconciliation gives us comfort, advice, and the assurance that our sins are forgotten. Life can now begin anew on the right – and often very different – track. We may or may not feel changed in the moment. But Christ means our reconciliation is simply a fact. And because we treasure our restored gift of closeness with God it changes what we say and do afterwards.

It may seem more odd to talk about being healed and not feeling it. When we are ill our deep desire is to feel better, and surely healing has no other point. True: but feeling better may take many forms. Our various ailments of body, mind and spirit are not simply undone in the sacrament of anointing. Instead, anointing for healing reorients us towards God. It reminds us of his infinite care for every detail of our lives. It renews our faith that we can trust God to do what is best for us, even if we do not understand it. God becomes again the source of our most real health and wellbeing. This does not mean neglecting science, and when God heals people it is mostly through doctors and medicines. But holy unction changes our perspective on our weakness. It transforms us into creatures who give thanks for whatever God sends us. We inhabit our bodies differently because once more we see our existence, however limited, as a beloved gift.

The joke is told of the congregation marvelling at one of their number who attends the Eucharist every day and receives Holy

Communion, and yet remains just as impossible to deal with. Indeed, the priest responds, but imagine what they would be like if they didn't come every day! Other sacraments are unique or occasional, but the sacrament of Christ's body and blood is our constant nourishment. We are what we eat. Little by little Christians cease to be simply bodies made of normal food and minds formed by careless influences. We become the body of Jesus himself. We find ourselves more and more acting with his actions and thinking with his mind (Phil. 2.5). This is not a smooth process. We experience setbacks and diversions. The world tries to feed everyone with the junk food of materialism and selfishness, and Christians are vulnerable to that too. But we keep on turning up – at least once a week, and perhaps every day – to receive the true, pure, life-giving food of unselfish love. Our deep desire to love like Christ is slowly transformed into the power to do exactly that.

In the end, all these sacramental transformations are refinements of the original, radical and definitive transformation. Baptism changes us from people who simply exist into people who are alive with real life, divine life. There is no bigger transformation than that. Perhaps we were baptized as infants and didn't choose for ourselves. No matter. When we make even a modest effort to live our baptism, we act out of the deepest desire of all. That is the desire to be whole, to be known, and to understand ourselves loved and capable of love. God gives us that desire, and he offers to fulfil it completely. We say yes to this offer by embracing baptism. And the perfect fulfilment of that desire comes about when we immerse ourselves in the sacramental life of God's Church. If we were baptized as infants, we receive confirmation as an adult sign of that commitment. In a commercial world it is easy to think that happiness depends on a lot of complex factors.

In fact, our most profound needs are very simple and are all met by God in the sacraments. We hear our sins forgiven, we feel Christ's healing touch. We know the fellowship of other Christians – for we cannot celebrate the Eucharist alone – and we taste God's own body and blood. Every part of who we are is caught up in the gradual and miraculous transformation God is working in us.

The psalmist says that God knows of what we are made. He knows that we are but dust. He knows we are not angels, or brains in vats, but animals, who need to be washed and stroked and fed. God is not waiting for us to somehow transcend the bodies he has given us. He loves us exactly as we are. God sends Jesus Christ among us as the pledge of that love. Through the sacraments God goes on sending Jesus Christ to us in every place and time and in every situation of human need and joy, to do over and over again what Christ first came to do: to call us, touch us, hold us, and bring us home.

Further Reading

Davison, Andrew (2013), *Why Sacraments?* London: SPCK.

Macquarrie, John (1997), *A Guide to the Sacraments*, London: SCM Press.

Quick, O. C. (1927), *The Christian Sacraments*, London: Nisbet & Co.

Schmemann, Alexander (1965), *The World as Sacrament*, London: Darton, Longman & Todd.

Waddell, Peter (2012), *Joy. The Meaning of the Sacraments*, Norwich: Canterbury Press.

10

Love Outspoken – Scripture and the Church

Jennifer Strawbridge

At a most basic level, Scripture is a collection of writings. These writings range in diversity across genres, cultures and perspectives. Written over a period of almost 1,000 years, they come from the ancient Mediterranean world which now encompasses what we call the Middle East, Turkey, Greece and Italy. Christians writing in the first few centuries spent much time and energy determining which writings should be considered Scripture, but we often assume that these books have always been together in the Bible. In fact, the Church drew these writings together over a period of about 300 years in order to uphold the message across all time that God is faithful and has raised Jesus from the dead. Christian Scripture – that which contains both the Old and New Testaments – is thus understood since the earliest centuries of Christianity as a coherent narrative.

What now demands our time and energy are not questions about the make-up of the Bible, but questions about how we are to interpret Scripture and how these texts impact our lives and our understanding of God. For example, if you were to drive around some parts of the United States, you might encounter this sticker on a car: 'God said it, I believe it, that settles it'. This phrase, referring most prominently to the words God 'says' in the Bible, is one way to shut down a difficult conversation about the inter-pretation of Scripture. In a disagreement over how we worship, or our politics, or our views on marriage, for example, to respond with 'that's what the Bible says and that settles it' effectively ends the conversation. Such a saying is the equivalent of a parent responding to a child's 'why' questions with the retort 'Because I said so.'

Without a doubt, when we read Scripture we interpret it by bringing our own opinions, hopes and judgements to the text. Some Christians believe that the Bible is God's word dictated to the writers. Others believe the Bible is inspired by God and the experience of God by God's people. Ultimately we don't believe in Scripture *per se*, we believe in the God that Scripture points us to and who we worship. Scripture tells the story of God's action in the creation of the world and in the judgement and redemption of that same world. And this is an essential point for how we make sense of Scripture within the Church.

This is also, however, where our initial definition of Scripture as a collection of writings begins to shift. Certainly, Scripture is a collection of texts, but it is also more than this for Christians. For a Christian, Scripture is God's word that reveals God's Word, who is Jesus Christ. This connection between God's word and the Word is most clear when we read the beginning of John's Gospel. Here we find that 'In the beginning was the Word, and the Word was with God, and the Word was God' (John 1.1). While the Gospels of Matthew and Luke begin with lengthy birth nar-ratives, elements of which make up Christmas pageants and crib services in churches every Advent and Christmas, John's Gospel begins with an introduction to the Word. John never tells us explicitly that the Word is Jesus, but it is pretty much impossible to assume otherwise. John continues that 'the Word became flesh and lived among us, and we have seen his glory, the glory as of a father's only son, full of grace and truth' (John 1.14). Through John's unique introduction to Jesus and his incarnation, through this Word who is both God and flesh, we know that one of the key titles given to Jesus is that of 'Word'. And so, when we say that Scripture is God's word that reveals God's Word to us, we are saying that Scripture reveals to us the work of God in the person of Jesus Christ.

What, then, are we to do with the reality that Christians across the centuries interpret parts of the Bible differently? For as long as texts have been called Scripture, this has been a concern. Within the Bible itself we find warnings for how a text is read, or misread, such as the admonition concerning Paul's letters that we find in 2 Peter. Here we find written that within all of Paul's letters, 'there are some things in them hard to understand, which the ignorant and unstable twist to their own destruction, as they do the other scriptures' (2 Peter 3.16). How we interpret – or misinterpret – Scripture is not a new problem.

One of the most influential early Christian writers to grapple with the interpretation of Scripture is a bishop named Augustine. He seeks the answer to the same question we do: What does it mean if I understand the text of the Bible in a way that is different from someone else? His response to this question is that in the study of Scripture 'all of us are trying to find and grasp the meaning of the author we are reading' (Augustine, 1991, 12.18.27). And yet this does not mean that for Augustine anything goes when it comes to reading Scripture. In fact, Augustine takes the interpretation of Scripture very seriously and struggles with what to do when he observes a text to have different meanings.

One example of Augustine's struggle comes in his very personal writing called the *Confessions*. Here, he spends pages upon pages writing about the beginning of the book of Genesis and the phrase 'in the beginning'. He discusses how this phrase can be understood both temporally – in terms of time and the nature of time itself – and logically – in terms of explaining the proper ordering of creation. Out of this lengthy discussion of what might appear to us to be three simple words – in the beginning – Augustine sets out his understanding of Scripture and how we are to read it. For Augustine, it is impossible to determine the exact meaning that the scriptural writer had in mind. Rather, only the Holy Spirit, who knows all truth, can help us to see the truth of a text. Even so, two readers of Scripture might put forward two different meanings of a text. Augustine's point is not that Scripture is contradictory or that it is an impenetrable mystery which we cannot know. His point is that when we read Scripture we cannot ultimately claim that the scriptural writer had *my* interpretation in mind.

The reason behind this claim is simple. The purpose of reading Scripture is not to ensure that the words of the text agree with our views and our opinions – something we will return to later in this chapter. Rather, the purpose of reading Scripture is to grow in our understanding of God and God's love. In this way, a number of so-called correct interpretations of Scripture exist. But for us to claim that we have the best interpretation means we are more focused on ourselves and getting it right than we are on the love of God, or perhaps on our neighbour who may read a text differently from us. The discussion of how to interpret the phrase 'in the beginning' is not simply about which understanding is the 'right' one. Ultimately, this phrase is about the story of a God who creates out of nothing 'in the beginning' in an eternal act of unending love. When it comes to our interpretation of Scripture, if the love of God and one another is sustained in our understanding of a text, this interpretation is a good one.

The active sense of Scripture revealing God's Word, whose presence and love is tangible in the words on each page, is emphasized throughout the biblical text. For example, the author of the book of Hebrews – one of the later texts in the New Testament – confirms this active nature of Scripture with the proclamation that 'the word of God is living and active' (Heb. 4.12). Such an understanding is essential to our interpretation of Scripture.

As Christians, we encounter Scripture as a living and active word. This leads many early Christians to compare Scripture to a human being, suggesting that just as humans are divided into different elements such as our flesh, our soul, and our spirit, so too is Scripture. Scripture is compared to the make-up of the human body as a living organism. What they mean by this is not as weird as it sounds, but brings us back to the question about different ways that we understand Scripture. There is, in this sense, a fleshly or literal understanding of Scripture, a soulful or ethical understanding, and a spiritual or allegorical understanding. In other words, Scripture as something living and active can be understood in a number of different senses. From this perspective, every Christian can read and interpret the biblical text and en- counter not only some level of meaning – bodily, soulful or spiritual – but also the revelation of God. By the power of the Spirit, Scripture reveals God to us.

Furthermore, the different active senses of Scripture are not intended to limit the text to one meaning. This isn't a neat way to solve the issue of different interpretations of a text. If we return to the story of creation and the language of 'in the beginning' we engaged earlier in this chapter, we can see how both the plain or literal sense of the text and the allegorical sense intersect. In the story of creation, we encounter an allegory of God's love in creating our world and seeing that 'it was good'. We can hold this understanding without ruling out an understanding of creation where God brings forth the world in a particular way (or ways, as we discovered in Chapter 3 on creation). One level of understanding does not negate the other. And yet the holding together of multiple meanings, and openness to the Spirit in our reading of Scripture, demands something more of us. It demands that we do not interpret Scripture in a vacuum.

Time and again in this book we have discovered that we cannot understand God in a vacuum and neither can we read Scripture in this way. Rather, Scripture is always to be read in the context of the Church of which we are a part, seeking the guidance of God the Holy Spirit, and shaped by our experience of worship and the sacraments. For example, the Church of England's services of Morning and Evening Prayer and its eucharistic services are made up almost entirely of the language of Scripture. 'O Lord, open our lips and our mouth shall proclaim your praise' is not only the opening acclamation of Morning Prayer, but is also the text of Psalm 51; the Lord's Prayer is taken from the Gospels of Matthew and Luke; 'Though we are many, we are one body, because we all share in one bread' is 1 Corinthians 10; and the concluding words of many services – 'The grace of our Lord Jesus Christ, and the love of God, and the fellowship of the Holy Spirit, be with us all evermore' – is from 2 Corinthians 13. Scripture infuses our services of worship.

We also read a lot of Scripture when we gather together in

prayer. The Daily Offices and services with the Eucharist use what is called a 'lectionary' which tells us what texts to read at each service. The lectionary ensures that over a period of no more than three years, we encounter almost the whole of the Bible. As such, through worship – through the liturgy – we are forced to engage with more than just our favourite passages, but also to grapple with the difficult texts. We encounter genocide, infanticide, rape, pillage and persecution. But alongside these difficult texts and the realities of sin, we also encounter the movement of the Holy Spirit and the revelation of God to those who love God.

Christian writer and scholar Derek Olsen writes that Scripture is 'the Church's book to be read paradigmatically within the Church's liturgy that brings us into deeper relationship with the God embodied, celebrated, and proclaimed within the Church' (Olsen, 2012). Reading Scripture, in other words, cannot be separated from the Church and community. Scripture can only be understood through the lens of love both of God and of neighbour and community. Therefore, anyone who thinks they have understood some part of Scripture but does not use this understanding to build up love of God and neighbour, has not actually understood that Scripture (Augustine, 1999, 1.36.40). In other words, all interpretation of Scripture must begin and end with love.

On the one hand, this understanding of Scripture and how we read it isn't difficult because the language of God's love permeates the Bible. We might think first and foremost of 1 Corinthians 13 where we are told that love is patient and kind, and that of faith, hope and love, 'the greatest of these is love' (1 Cor. 13.13). Or we might immediately turn to John 3.16 where we are told that 'God so loved the world that he gave his only Son'. But God's love spans the whole of Scripture. Thus, we find descriptions of God's love in Zephaniah where we are told that God 'will rejoice over you with gladness, he will renew you in his love' (Zeph. 3.17) and in the Psalms where God is 'abounding in steadfast love to all who call on you' (Ps. 86.5). We are commanded in John's Gospel to 'abide' in God's love (John 15.9), told in Romans that 'God proves his love for us in that while we still were sinners Christ died for us' (Rom. 5.8), and reminded time and again in 1 John to love God and one another 'because God is love' (1 John 4.8). The love of God is the lens through which we are to interpret Scripture and it is also what permeates the biblical text. And thus, throughout Scripture we learn that God's love is unchanging, steadfast, revealed through Christ, poured into our hearts through the Holy Spirit, and is what moves us to love one another.

On the other hand, interpreting Scripture through the lens of love is extremely difficult because it forces us to come face to face with the expectations and assumptions that we bring to Scripture. What if the interpretation we want to find means excluding our neighbour from the love of God or ours? Interpretation is never free from our own expectations, which is why our task in reading Scripture is both to seek the love of God, and not to find our own opinions and assumptions confirmed. Using Scripture simply to confirm our presuppositions is 'an act of resistance against God's fresh speaking to us, an effective denial that the Bible is the word of the living God' (Davis, 2003, p. 16). It is a denial of the living and active nature of God's word and God's Word. In reading Scripture, we are called to be open to transformation, and to change both our minds and our lives. We must not be conformed to our own opinions, 'but be transformed by the renewing of your minds, so that you may discern what is the will of God – what is good and acceptable and perfect' (Rom. 12.2). In other words, we must discern God's good and perfect love. When we read

Scripture, we behold the glory of God within God's very word and when we do, we find ourselves 'transformed into the same image from one degree of glory to another' (2 Cor. 3.18). And that 'image' is none other than Christ. What is at stake, therefore, when we encounter Scripture is not our views and our opinions and whether they are right or sound, but our salvation.

Within the traditions of the Church of England and within ordination services across the globe, we find the statement that Scripture 'contains all things necessary for salvation'. Scripture reveals God's Word to us and that Word is the means of our salvation. Scripture is God's revelation of God's very self for our salvation through faith in Christ and through the faithfulness of Christ. We read Scripture to learn about God's relationship to humankind from the beginning, in the context of the Church which is the body of Christ, for the Word (Christ) who we come to know and love through God's word (Scripture) is the one who draws us into the realm of God's infinite love.

This understanding of Scripture is difficult to fit onto a car sticker so that we might counter the phrase with which we started: 'God said it, I believe it, that settles it'. The words of Scripture are not intended to end conversations, but to begin them because Scripture is always an invitation to enter more deeply into the love of God. And this invitation into God's love never ends in this life for, as St Augustine concludes, when it comes to Scripture, even 'if I had tried to apply myself to it exclusively from my earliest childhood to extreme old age, spending all my free time on it, all my effort, and if I had had a better gift of mind', there would still be new treasures and meanings to discover each and every day (Augustine, *Letter* 137, 1.3; in Augustine, 2010).

Further Reading

Bartlett, David (1999), *Between the Bible and the Church*, Nashville, TN: Abingdon Press.

Chadwick, Henry (2009), *Augustine of Hippo: A Life*, Oxford: Oxford University Press.

Dunn, James D. G. (1987), *The Living Word*, London: SCM Press.

Riches, John K. (2000), *The Bible: A Very Short Introduction*, Oxford: Oxford University Press.

References

Chapter 1

Burrows, Ruth (2012), *Love Unknown*, London: Bloomsbury.

McCabe, Herbert (1999), *God Matters*, London: Bloomsbury.

Williams, Rowan (2012), *Being Christian*, London: SPCK.

Chapter 2

Berry, Wendell (2012), 'Manifesto: The Mad Farmer Liberation Front' in *New Collected Poems*, Berkeley: Counterpoint, pp. 173–4.

Groves, Peter (2018), 'The Trinity: The Basis of Christian Life', available at: www.theschooloftheology.org/posts/essay/on-the-trinity-2018 [accessed 24 May 2018].

Chapter 3

Plato (1929), *Timaeus. Critias. Cleitophon. Menexenus. Epistles*, trans. R. G. Bury, Loeb Classical Library 234, Cambridge, MA: Harvard University Press.

Westminster Assembly (1986), *The Westminster Shorter Catechism in Modern English*, Phillipsburg, NJ: Presbyterian and Reformed Publishing Company.

Chapter 5

Barth, Karl (1960), *The Humanity of God*, trans. John Newton Thomas, Louisville, KT: Westminster John Knox Press.

Williams, Rowan (2000), *On Christian Theology*, Oxford: Blackwell.

Williams, Rowan (2015), *What Is Christianity?* London: SPCK.

Chapter 8

Alison, James (1993), *Knowing Jesus, London: SPCK.*

O'Collins, Gerald (2013), *Christology: A Biblical, Historical, and Systematic Study of Jesus*, Oxford: Oxford University Press.

Chapter 10

Augustine (1991), *Confessions*, trans. Henry Chadwick, Oxford: Oxford University Press.

Augustine (1999), *On Christian Teaching*, trans. R.P.H. Green, Oxford: Oxford University Press.

Augustine (2010), *Augustine in His Own Words*, trans. and ed. William I. Harmless, Washington DC: Catholic University of America Press.

Davis, Ellen F. (2003), 'Teaching the Bible Confessionally in the Church' in Ellen F. Davis and Richard B. Hays (eds), *The Art of Reading Scripture*, Grand Rapids, MI: Eerdmans, pp. 9–26.

Davis, Ellen F. and Hays, Richard B. (eds) (2003), *The Art of Reading Scripture*, Grand Rapids, MI: Eerdmans.

Olsen, Derek (2012), 'Academic Reading and Devotional Reading of the Bible', available at: www.stbedeproductions.com/academic-reading-and-devotional-reading-of-the-bible/ (accessed 10 July 2018).

Index

INDEX

INDEX

INDEX